HOME COOKING

MW01408908

Family Favorites

WQED
Multimedia
PITTSBURGH

A production of WQED Multimedia

WQED
Multimedia
PITTSBURGH

For other great merchandise, visit Shop WQED at
www.wqed.org, or call 1-800-274-1307, or write to
SHOP WQED, 4802 Fifth Avenue, Pittsburgh, PA 15213

For WQED Multimedia:

Executive Vice President & General Manager
Deborah L. Acklin

Vice President, Business & Finance
Patty Walker

Director, Distribution & Client Services
Keyola Panza

Manager, Product Sales & Operations
Robyn Martin

America's Home Cooking Producer/Host
Chris Fennimore

Art Director
Dave Rohm

Cookbook Editor
Joyce DeFrancesco

Illustration
Maryann Fennimore

Table of Contents

APPETIZERS AND BRUNCH

Apple Cheddar Quiche 10

Balzamaca (Croatian Corn
Bread) 11

Breakfast Casserole 12

Cheese Pockets 13

Chicken Poppers 14

Chocolate Chip Cheese Spread . . .15

Dippy Cheese Fondue 16

Easy Special Breakfast Bowl 17

Grandma Rutherford's Checkerboard
Biscuits 18

Hungarian Butter 19

Nutty Baked French Toast 20

Pancake in the Oven 21

Party Sausage 22

Pineapple Casserole 23

Sauerkraut Balls 24

Spinach Dip 25

Stuffed French Toast 26

Taco Pie Quiche 27

*Tortilla Espanola (Spanish
Omelet) 28

Turkey Sausage Wonton
Appetizer .29

SALADS AND SOUPS

Baba's Slovak Mushroom Soup . . .32

Blue Cheese Salad 33

Broccoli/Cheese Soup 34

Brodoso (Italian Chicken Soup) . . .35

Chicken, Black Bean, Corn & Tomato
Salad 36

Curried Fruit & Nut Salad 37

Easter Salad 38

Easy Chicken Rivel Soup 39

French Chicken Salad 40

Grandma Perskey's Cabbage
Soup 41

Grandma's French Dressing 42

Grandma's Vegetable Soup 43

Green Bean and Potato Soup 44

Italian Macaroni Salad 45

Langostino Corn Chowder 46

Lemon Glazed Fruit Salad 47

Lime Cheese Salad 48

* Recipes were prepared on "America's Home Cooking: Family Favorites"

Table of Contents

Old-Fashioned Potato Salad 49

Special Spinach Salad 50

Tortellini Soup 51

Tuscan Sausage Soup 52

Vegetable Beef Soup 53

Veggie Potato Salad 54

PASTA AND POTATOES

Angelic Sweet Potatoes 58

Artichoke Stuffed Manicotti 59

Au Gratin Potatoes 60

Aunt Helen's Baked Spaghetti 61

Baked Perciatelli 62

Bobalki (Slovak Christmas Eve
Dish) 63

Brother-in-Law Rigatoni Sosso . . .64

Butternut Squash Gnocchi with
Sage 65

Donna's Italian Pasta Stew 66

Haluski Drop Dumplings (Grated
Potatoes) .67

Nonna's Broccoli and Pasta 68

Noodle Bake 69

Penne Alla Noci 70

Perogie Casserole 71

Potato Balls 72

Potato Dumplings and Kraut 73

Potato Latkes 74

Rice Pilaf .75

Ricotta Gnocchi 76

Ricotta Sauce with Walnuts 77

Rigatoni with Spinach-Ricotta
Filling 78

Risotto 79

Scalloped Potatoes 80

Scalloped Potatoes Parmesan 81

*Scrippelles (Crepes) 82

Sister Mary Francis' Potatoes 83

Spaghetti Casserole 84

Spaghetti Pizza 85

Spanish Rice 86

Sweet Potato Casserole 87

Turkey Lasagna 88

* Recipes were prepared on "America's Home Cooking: Family Favorites"

3

Table of Contents

ENTREES

Apricot Chicken 92

Baba's Sausage Bake 93

Baccala Alla Manuella 94

Barbecued Hamburgers 95

Barnesboro Tavern Burgers 96

Beanless Chili 97

Big Sandwich, The 98

Bourbon Baked Ham 99

Braciole .100

Bracoli 101

Chicken Elegance 102

Chicken Enchilada Casserole 103

Chicken Lo Mein 104

Chicken Loaf 105

Chicken with Rice & Pignolia
Nuts 106

Dad's Famous Slop 107

Dad's Ham/Potato Casserole 108

Eye of Round Roast 109

Grandma Tippy-Toe's Swiss
Steak 110

Grandma's Meatloaf 111

Ham Balls 112

Ham Hawaiian 113

Ham Loaf 114

Hobo Stew 115

Huffle Puffle 116

Italian Shepherd Pie 117

Johnny Mayette, Revisited 118

Karin's Chicken Divan 119

*Kennywood Picnic City Chicken
Sticks 120

Mazetti 121

Meatloaf Japanese Style 122

Missouri .123

Mustard Chicken or One-Pot
Chicken .124

Oven-Fried Chicken 125

Pan De Elote 126

Paprika Schnitzel 127

Pastor Matt's Shepherd Pie 128

Polpette .129

Pork Chops with Ketchup 130

* Recipes were prepared on "America's Home Cooking: Family Favorites"

Table of Contents

Pork Snitzel 131

Pork-Q-Pine Balls 132

Real Gone Barbecued Pot
Roast 133

Saturday Buried Treasure 134

Sauerkraut Casserole 135

Sicilian Steak 136

Slow Cooked Glazed Ham 137

*Spiedini 138

Steak, Bacon & Macaroni 139

Stuffed Bread 140

Stuffed Cabbage 141

Stuffed Peppers European
Style 142

Sweet and Sour Meatballs with
Cabbage 143

Swiss Smoked Turkey Bake 144

Szekely Gulyas 145

Tangy Pork Chops 146

Turkey Tetrazinni 147

Unstuffed Cabbage Casserole . . .148

Upside Down Pizza Pie 149

VEGETABLES

Baked Mushroom Casserole 152

Broccoli Casserole 153

Eggplant Casserole 154

English Walnut Broccoli 155

Gardener's Special Platter 156

Great Aunt Margaret Tarr's Cheesy
Vegetables 157

Italian Green Beans 158

Leeks with Olive Oil (a la Turk) . . .159

Mom's Zucchini Casserole 160

*Nanna's Eggplant Patties 161

Onions Oliver 162

Stuffed Artichokes 163

Sweet and Sour Green Beans . . .164

Vegetable Bake 165

DESSERTS AND SWEETS

7 Up Pound Cake 168

Anise Cakes 169

Apple Pie in a Bag 170

Apricot Lemon Marmalade 171

* Recipes were prepared on "America's Home Cooking: Family Favorites"

Table of Contents

Baklava 172

*Bishop's Bread 173

Black Magic Cake with Whipped
Cream Icing 174

Black Walnut Cookies 175

Brown Pudding 176

Butterscotch Pie 177

Caramel Dumplings 178

Carrot Cupcakes 179

*Cassava Cake 180

Cay's Killer Cheesecake 181

*Cheesecake 182

Chewy Chocolate Cookies 183

Chocolate Cheesecake 184

Chocolate Chippers 185

Chocolate Feather Pudding 186

Co-Co Cappuccino Cheesecake . .187

Coconut Macaroons 188

Cranberry Pistachio Biscotti 189

Danish Apple Pastry 190

Fruit and Coconut Dessert
Dumplings 191

Fudge Crackles 192

Gram's Gingerbread Men 193

Grandma's Apple Butter Pie 194

Grandma's Nut Rolls 195

Grossmutter's Schmerkase
Pie 196

Honeyed Applesauce 197

Key Lime Pie 198

Killarney Bread 199

Lemon Zucchini Bread 200

Mandel Bread 201

Mint Chocolate Angel Food
Cake 202

Molasses Sugar Cookies 203

Ninety-Minute Dinner Rolls 204

Noodle Pudding 205

Palachinka (Croatian Crepes) 206

Peanut Butter Pie 207

*Pignoli Cookies 208

Polish Pound Cake 209

Poor Man's Cake 210

* Recipes were prepared on "America's Home Cooking: Family Favorites"

Table of Contents

Puto or Philippine Steamed
Bread 211

Reese's Peanut Butter Cake 212

Saucy Peach Cobbler 213

Spritz Cookies 214

Strawberry Dream Dessert 215

Sugar Cookies with Icing 216

Sunny Strawberry Soup 217

Texas Sheet Cake 218

White Chocolate Crunch 219

Yummy Cake 220

Zazvorniky (Slovak Ginger
Cookies) .221

Index 222-227

* Recipes were prepared on "America's Home Cooking: Family Favorites"

FAMILY FAVORITES

Appetizers and Brunch

Apple Cheddar Quiche

DIRECTIONS

Preheat oven to 350 degrees. Scald milk and then let cool. Moisten pie shell with 1 egg white. Whip eggs with cinnamon and nutmeg. Mix apple wedges with the seasoned eggs and cheese. Pour into shell and bake for 45 minutes.

INGREDIENTS

1 cup milk

1 (9-inch) pie shell

1 egg white

3 eggs

1 teaspoon cinnamon

1 teaspoon nutmeg

1 apple, cut into bite-sized wedges

2/3 cup cheddar cheese

SUBMITTED BY:
Laura Nowakowski, Pittsburgh

America's
HOME COOKING

Balzamaca
(Croatian Corn Bread)

DIRECTIONS

Preheat oven to 350 degrees. Mix all ingredients together. Grease a 9x13-inch pan with butter or cooking spray and pour ingredients into it. Bake for 1 hour.

INGREDIENTS

1/2 cup flour

1/2 cup cornmeal

8 eggs

1 1/3 cup granulated sugar

2 1/2 tablespoons baking powder

2 1/2 cups buttermilk

1 cup sour cream

1 pound cottage cheese

1/2 cup (1 stick) butter, melted

SUBMITTED BY:
Mary Kocian & Josephine Kocian Crame,
Reserve

America's HOME COOKING

11

Breakfast Casserole

DIRECTIONS

Mix together eggs, milk, taco seasoning and soup. In a 9x11-inch glass pan, layer the cooked sausage with the croutons. Pour egg mixture on top and sprinkle on cheese. Refrigerate overnight. Bake at 350 degrees for 1 hour or until done.

NOTE

A mix of hot and country-style bulk sausage from the deli is an excellent choice for this recipe.

INGREDIENTS

12 eggs

1 cup milk

1 package taco seasoning mix

1 (10 1/2-ounce) can cream of mushroom soup

1 pound sausage, browned

1 (6-ounce) box seasoned croutons

2 cups shredded cheese

SUBMITTED BY:
Ellen Matthews, Greensburg

Cheese Pockets

DIRECTIONS

Preheat oven to 350 degrees. Mix cheeses and eggs together. Cover all phyllo dough sheets with a damp cloth, as directed by directions on box. Butter each sheet, one at a time, before filling it with the egg and cheese mixture. (Keep other sheets covered with damp cloth until ready to fill.) Fold each sheet into thirds. Place a heaping teaspoon of the cheese mixture on the left end of the folded phyllo sheet. Fold the filled phyllo sheet into a 3-inch triangle. (Keep flipping the dough over to form the 3-inch triangle—this action forms the layers of phyllo.) Brush each triangle with melted butter and place on an ungreased cookie sheet. Bake for 15 minutes until brown. Makes 40 cheese pockets.

INGREDIENTS

1 (8-ounce) package cream cheese

2 (8-ounce) packages farmer's or ricotta cheese

1/4 pound plain, crumbled feta cheese

1 to 2 eggs, depending on thickness of cheese mixture

1 (16-ounce) box phyllo dough sheets

1/2 pound butter, melted

SUBMITTED BY:
An'ge Ross Sassos, Greensburg

America's
HOME COOKING

Chicken Poppers

DIRECTIONS

Flatten chicken breasts to 1/4-inch thickness and cut into 1 1/2-inch strips. Spread each strip with 1 teaspoon of ground ham. Place a cheese cube on the end of each strip and roll up. Cut each slice of bacon in half width-wise. Wrap a piece of bacon around each chicken roll-up and secure with a toothpick. In a large skillet, cook roll-ups in olive oil until bacon is crispy, about 10 minutes. Add broth, salt and pepper; bring to a boil. Reduce heat, cover and simmer for 10 to 15 minutes.

INGREDIENTS

3 pounds boneless, skinless chicken breasts

1 cup ground fully-cooked ham

25 to 30 1/2-inch cheddar cheese cubes

1 pound sliced bacon

3 tablespoons olive oil

1 cup chicken broth

1/2 teaspoon salt

1/2 teaspoon pepper

SUBMITTED BY:
Betty Pandullo, Blairsville

Chocolate Chip Cheese Spread

DIRECTIONS

In a medium mixing bowl, beat the cream cheese, butter and vanilla until fluffy. Gradually add sugars, beat until just combined. Stir in chocolate chips. Spread on chocolate graham crackers. Makes 2 cups.

INGREDIENTS

1 (8-ounce) package cream cheese, softened

1/2 cup butter, softened

1/4 teaspoon pure vanilla extract

3/4 cup confectioners' sugar

2 tablespoons brown sugar

3/4 cup mini semi-sweet chocolate chips

Chocolate graham crackers, for serving

SUBMITTED BY:
Bonnie Mortimer, Mt. Pleasant

Dippy Cheese Fondue

DIRECTIONS

Preheat oven to 250 degrees. Rub the inside of a medium, nonstick saucepan with garlic. Add wine and set over medium heat. When wine is hot, but not boiling, add lemon juice. Toss cheese with flour. Add cheese mixture to saucepan one handful at a time, stirring constantly with a wooden spoon until melted and smooth. Bring mixture to a slow boil, add optional kirsch and spices. Stir until well blended and thickened. Toast bread cubes in oven for 10 minutes. Sauté ham cubes in 2 teaspoons vegetable oil until lightly browned. Peel, core and slice apples. Blanche broccoli in salted boiling water for 1 minute then rinse under cold water. Serve bread, ham, apples and broccoli with fondue.

NOTE

1/2 pound each of emmenthaler and gruyere cheeses may be substituted for the Swiss cheese.

INGREDIENTS

1 clove garlic, peeled and halved

1 3/4 cup dry white wine

1 tablespoon fresh lemon juice

1 pound Swiss cheese

3 tablespoons flour

3 tablespoons kirsch, German cherry brandy (optional)

1/2 teaspoon nutmeg

1/4 teaspoon pepper

1/4 teaspoon paprika

1 loaf Italian or French bread, cut into 1-inch cubes

1 pound cooked ham, cut into 1-inch cubes

2 teaspoons vegetable oil

2 Granny Smith apples

1 pound broccoli, cut into bite-sized pieces and blanched, for serving

SUBMITTED BY:
Jim Baran, Pittsburgh

Easy Special Breakfast Bowl

DIRECTIONS

Prepare country gravy in medium saucepan using 1 cup milk and 1/2 cup water. Stir and bring to gentle boil. Add cooked crumbled sausage and simmer 2 minutes. Remove from burner and cover to keep warm. Heat frozen sausage patties according to directions. Keep warm. Fry eggs over easy in melted butter or margarine or spray. Meanwhile, lightly toast muffin halves. Butter toasted muffins. In individual bowls, place a muffin half and top with warm sausage patty, cheese slice, fried egg and second muffin half. Pour hot sausage gravy over each serving. Serves 4.

NOTE

If preferred, substitute sliced Canadian bacon, capicola or sliced deli baked ham for the sausage patties. Eliminate both meats for a vegetarian meal. For extra ease, use canned or frozen sausage gravy and heat according to directions.

INGREDIENTS

1 (2 1/2-ounce) package country gravy mix

1 cup milk

1/2 cup water

1/2 pound sausage, cooked and crumbled

4 frozen precooked sausage patties

4 large eggs

Butter or margarine

4 English muffins, split

4 slices American cheese

SUBMITTED BY:
Chris Bobick, Chalk Hill

17

Grandma Rutherford's Checkerboard Biscuits

DIRECTIONS

Preheat oven to 450 degrees. Mix each biscuit separately, but in the same manner: Mix dry ingredients and cut shortening in until dough resembles coarse cornmeal. Stir in milk. Pat out biscuits to about 1/2 inch high. Cut biscuits and place next to each other in a checkerboard pattern on an ungreased cookie sheet. Bake for 10 to 12 minutes, or until done. Serve with raspberry preserves or orange marmalade.

INGREDIENTS

DARK BISCUITS:

2 cups minus 6 tablespoons flour

4 teaspoons baking powder

1/4 cup sugar

6 tablespoons cocoa powder

1/2 teaspoon salt

1/2 teaspoon cream of tartar

1/2 cup shortening

2/3 cup milk

LIGHT BISCUITS:

2 cups flour

4 teaspoons baking powder

6 teaspoons sugar

1/2 teaspoon salt

1/2 teaspoon cream of tartar

1/2 cup shortening

2/3 cup milk

Raspberry preserves or orange marmalade, for serving

SUBMITTED BY:

Leslie Rutherford, Clairton

America's HOME COOKING

Hungarian Butter

DIRECTIONS

Beat first 4 ingredients with mixer in a large glass cup. When mixture is the consistency of whipped cream, add 1 teaspoon of caraway seeds by rubbing them between palms of hands. Beat mixture again and refrigerate. When ready to serve, let stand at room temperature for 15 to 30 minutes. Place in decorative bowl and sprinkle with paprika. Serve on toasted onion or butter crackers.

INGREDIENTS

1/4 pound butter, softened to room temperature

1 (8-ounce) package cream cheese

1 teaspoon dark or spicy mustard

1 small onion, very finely chopped

1 teaspoon caraway seed

Paprika, for garnishing

Toasted onion or butter crackers, for serving

SUBMITTED BY:
Pamela Glaser, Wilkinsburg

Nutty Baked French Toast

DIRECTIONS

Generously grease 13x9-inch pan. Fill pan with bread slices to within 1/2 inch of top. Blend together eggs, milk, half & half, nutmeg, vanilla and cinnamon. Pour over bread slices. Cover and refrigerate overnight. Combine topping ingredients and set aside until ready to bake toast. (Topping can be refrigerated overnight as well.) When ready to bake, preheat oven to 350 degrees. Briefly soften topping in the microwave and spread over toast. Bake for 50 minutes until puffed and golden.

NOTE

To make for easier clean up, put a cookie sheet under the pan in the oven in case the toast boils over. If the top of the toast browns too quickly, cover with foil.

INGREDIENTS

1 loaf white bread, sliced

8 eggs

2 cups milk

2 cups half & half

1/2 teaspoon nutmeg

2 teaspoons vanilla

1/2 teaspoon cinnamon

NUT TOPPING:

3/4 cup butter, softened

1 1/3 cups brown sugar

3 tablespoons dark corn syrup

1 1/3 cups coarsely chopped walnuts

SUBMITTED BY:
Mary Dawson, Poland

America's
HOME COOKING

Pancake in the Oven

DIRECTIONS

Preheat oven to 350 degrees. Mix milk, flour and sugar. Add eggs. Spread some bacon grease in a 9x13-inch pan. Pour mixture into pan. Add bacon. Bake for 1 hour or until brown.

INGREDIENTS

2 cups milk

1 cup flour

2 teaspoons sugar

3 eggs

Bacon grease

1 pound bacon, cooked and diced

SUBMITTED BY:
Felicia Richards, North Huntingdon

Party Sausage

DIRECTIONS

Mix all ingredients together. Cook in a slow cooker on low for 6 to 7 hours or in a pot on the stove for 1 hour.

INGREDIENTS

3/4 cup bourbon

1 1/2 cup ketchup

1/2 cup brown sugar

1 tablespoon onion

1 teaspoon oregano

1 teaspoon rosemary

2 to 3 pounds smoked sausage

SUBMITTED BY:
Julie Robb, Elizabeth

America's
HOME COOKING

Pineapple Casserole

DIRECTIONS

Preheat oven to 350 degrees. Butter or grease a 2-quart casserole dish. In a mixing bowl, blend together sugar and flour. Add pineapple and cheese; mix well and pour into casserole dish. Mix butter and cracker crumbs. Sprinkle top with cracker mixture and bake for 30 to 40 minutes.

INGREDIENTS

1/2 cup white sugar

1/4 tablespoon all-purpose flour

3 (20-ounce) cans pineapple chunks, drained

2 cups shredded longhorn cheese

1/4 pound butter, melted

25 round butter crackers, crumbled

SUBMITTED BY:
Katie Manni, Atlasburg

23

Sauerkraut Balls

DIRECTIONS

Preheat oven to 375 degrees. Brown sausage and onion in skillet; drain. Add sauerkraut and 2 tablespoons breadcrumbs. In smaller bowl, combine cream cheese, parsley, mustard, garlic salt and pepper. Stir into kraut mixture; chill. Once chilled, shape mixture into small balls. Coat balls with flour. Add milk to beaten eggs and dip balls into egg mixture. Roll balls in breadcrumbs and fry them in vegetable oil until brown. Drain on paper towels and then bake balls for 15 to 20 minutes.

INGREDIENTS

8 ounces ground sausage

1/4 cup finely chopped onion

1 (14-ounce) can sauerkraut, drained and snipped

2 tablespoons dry breadcrumbs

1 (3-ounce) package cream cheese, softened

2 tablespoons parsley

1 teaspoon mustard

Dash of garlic salt

1/4 teaspoon pepper

1/4 cup all-purpose flour

1/4 cup milk

2 eggs, well beaten

1 cup breadcrumbs

SUBMITTED BY:
Amy Kelly, North Hills

America's
HOME COOKING

Spinach Dip

DIRECTIONS

Combined first 7 ingredients in a large mixing bowl; mix thoroughly until blended. Scoop out center of sweet bread; pour mixture into bread. Cut scooped-out portion of bread for dipping.

INGREDIENTS

1 (10-ounce) package chopped frozen spinach, thawed

1 (16-ounce) container low-fat sour cream

1 (16-ounce) jar low-fat mayonnaise

1 package dry vegetable soup mix

1 (8-ounce) can water chestnuts

Green onions, diced

Sliced almonds, diced

1 loaf sweet bread

SUBMITTED BY:
Paul Fronczek, Pittsburgh

25

Stuffed French Toast

DIRECTIONS

Pour 4 cups of croutons in bottom of greased 9x13-inch casserole. Slice or cube cream cheese and layer over croutons. Use remaining croutons to form top layer. Beat eggs, syrup, milk and cinnamon together. Pour over croutons and cream cheese layers. Sprinkle lightly with more cinnamon. Cover and refrigerate overnight. Bake, covered, at 375 degrees for 45 minutes. Let sit 10 to 15 minutes before cutting. Serve with warm syrup.

INGREDIENTS

8 cups plain croutons

1 to 2 (8-ounce) packages cream cheese

12 eggs

1/2 cup maple syrup

2 cups milk

1 teaspoon cinnamon

Warm syrup, for serving

SUBMITTED BY:
Andrea Gambrel, Poland

Taco Pie Quiche

DIRECTIONS

Preheat oven to 375 degrees. Brown beef in skillet; drain fat. Stir in water and taco seasoning. Cover and simmer, following package directions. Cool mixture for 10 minutes. Add cheese and chilies and mix well. Spoon into preheated pastry shell. Combine eggs, cream and salt; mix until smooth. Pour over meat mixture. Bake for 40 to 45 minutes or until custard is set and pastry is browned. Allow pie to stand 5 minutes before serving.

INGREDIENTS

1/2 pound ground beef

1/2 cup water

1/2 package taco seasoning mix

1/2 cup shredded monterey jack cheese

2 ounces green chilies, seeded and diced

1 (9-inch) prebaked pastry shell, preheated

3 eggs

1 cup light cream

Salt, to taste

SUBMITTED BY:
Sharon Lemasters, Morgantown

27

Tortilla Espanola (Spanish Omelet)

DIRECTIONS

Sauté onion slices in 2 tablespoons olive oil over medium-high heat in a nonstick pan. Sauté onions until very soft and some slices are browned and caramelized. Remove onions from pan when done and set aside. Peel potatoes and cut into quarters; thinly slice each quarter. Place sliced potatoes in a microwave-safe bowl, add 2 tablespoons oil and 1 1/2 teaspoons of salt. Mix by hand until well blended. Microwave potatoes on high for 1 1/2 minutes. Add potatoes to same pan used for onions. Sauté until edges brown. Turn heat to low, add onions and mix well, spreading mixture evenly in pan. Beat eggs; add milk, 1/2 teaspoon salt, black pepper and paprika. Add eggs to potatoes and onions. Turn heat to medium and cover. Let cook until just a small amount of liquid remains on top. Firmly place a large flat plate on the pan (the plate should cover the pan). Place palm firmly on the plate and flip the pan so that the plate is on the bottom. Gently slide the omelet back onto the pan with the uncooked side on the bottom. Turn heat to low and cook for 1 minute. Clean plate and again place firmly on the pan. Flip omelet, slice and serve warm.

INGREDIENTS

1 large onion, thinly sliced

3 medium potatoes

4 large eggs

2 tablespoons milk

Olive oil

2 teaspoons salt

1/4 teaspoon black pepper

1/4 teaspoon paprika (optional)

SUBMITTED BY:
Sheena Jacob, Swissvale

28

Turkey Sausage Wonton Appetizer

DIRECTIONS

Preheat oven to 350 degrees. Remove casing from sausage. Cook sausage and green peppers; drain. Add olives, ranch dressing and cheese. Place 2x2-inch wonton wrappers into a 12-hole nut cup pan. Run a finger around the wrapper to fit it inside the hole and fill the wrapper with 2 teaspoons of the sausage mixture. Bake until cheese melts and tips of wrappers are light brown. Makes 2 dozen appetizers.

NOTE

The sausage mixture can be prepared a day ahead if desired.

INGREDIENTS

1 pound hot turkey sausage

1 large green pepper, diced

1/2 cup black olives, diced

1 (8-ounce) bottle ranch dressing

1 (8-ounce) package shredded 4-cheese blend

1 (12-ounce) package wonton wrappers

SUBMITTED BY:
Barbara Heyman, Conway

America's
HOME COOKING

America's

HOME COOKING

FAMILY FAVORITES

Salads and Soups

Baba's Slovak Mushroom Soup

DIRECTIONS

Rinse dried porcini mushrooms in a colander and put dried mushrooms in a large bowl. Cover with hot water. Let mushrooms sit in hot water for about 30 to 60 minutes. With a paper towel or coffee filter, line a strainer or colander and place over large bowl or pot and drain mushrooms. Save the mushroom water. Chop mushrooms and strain mushroom water again; set mushroom water aside. Using an 8- or 12-quart stock pot, melt butter and sauté the celery and onion. When celery and onion begin to soften, add the parsley and chopped porcini, portobello and button mushrooms. Cover pot and sauté for a few minutes until mushrooms cook down. Add saved mushroom water; add more water to fill pot about 3/4 full. Add bouillon cubes and salt and pepper to taste. Cook about 45 minutes. In a separate pot, cook egg flake noodles according to package directions. When ready to serve, add noodles to soup.

NOTE

Recipe also can be made with a mix and match of any variety of fresh mushrooms.

SUBMITTED BY:
Sharon Morgano, North Versailles

INGREDIENTS

Dried porcini mushrooms

1/2 cup (1 stick) butter

4 ribs of celery, including leaves, chopped

1 medium onion, chopped

Fresh parsley, chopped

2 portobello mushroom caps, cleaned and chopped

1 pound button mushrooms, chopped

5 vegetable bouillon cubes, or a mixture of vegetable and beef cubes

Salt, to taste

Pepper, to taste

1 (12-ounce) bag egg flake noodles

America's HOME COOKING

Blue Cheese Salad

DIRECTIONS

Mix all dressing ingredients and store in refrigerator. (Dressing tastes best if refrigerated for 1 day.)

To make salad, combine lettuce, eggs, croutons and 1/2 of the dressing. Mix well. Increase dressing until desired taste and consistency is reached.

INGREDIENTS

1 head lettuce, torn into small pieces

4 eggs, hard boiled and broken up with a fork

1 (5- or 6-ounce) package seasoned croutons

DRESSING:

1 (4-ounce) package crumbled blue cheese

2 cups mayonnaise

1/2 cup water

2 tablespoons cider vinegar

1 small onion, very finely diced

SUBMITTED BY:
Andrea Gambrel, Poland

Broccoli/Cheese Soup

DIRECTIONS

Combine broccoli, potatoes, onion, water, salt and pepper; cook for 25 minutes. Add cheese and soups and cook an additional 20 minutes.

INGREDIENTS

20 ounces chopped broccoli

2 cups cubed potatoes

1 medium onion, chopped

5 cups water

Salt and pepper, to taste

1 pound pasteurized process cheese

1 (10 1/2-ounce) can cream of chicken soup

1 (10 1/2-ounce) can cream of celery soup

SUBMITTED BY:
Julie Robb, Elizabeth

Brodoso
(Italian Chicken Soup)

DIRECTIONS

Cook chicken in 3 cups water for 20 to 30 minutes; skim and discard residue that comes to the surface. Remove chicken and set aside for later. Strain broth and set aside. In a large soup pot, sauté onions and celery in olive oil until soft. Add garlic and continue to cook for 1 to 2 minutes. Add basil, tomatoes and beans, including liquid in can. Add strained chicken broth, paste soup base and 3 to 4 cans of water (use empty bean cans). Bring to boil, then lower heat to low and simmer for 1 hour. Meanwhile, pull chicken apart into bite-size pieces and add to soup. Squeeze water out of thawed spinach and add to soup, breaking apart with fingers. Add salt and pepper, to taste. Simmer for about 30 minutes; soup should be very thick. Cook soup noodles separately, drain and serve in a separate bowl, allowing guests to add noodles to their soup. Sprinkle grated parmesan cheese over individual bowls to serve.

INGREDIENTS

2 boneless, skinless chicken breasts

2 to 3 tablespoons olive oil

1 large onion, chopped

5 to 6 celery stalks with leaves, chopped

1 clove garlic, mashed, or 1/4 teaspoon garlic powder

4 to 5 fresh basil leaves, chopped, or 1/2 teaspoon dried basil

1 (14 1/2-ounce) can diced tomatoes, with juice

2 (15-ounce) cans cannellini beans

4 tablespoons paste chicken stock base or 4 chicken bouillon cubes

1 (10-ounce) package frozen spinach, thawed

Salt and pepper, to taste

Cooked ditalini, acini de pepe or other small soup noodle, for serving

Grated parmesan cheese, for serving

SUBMITTED BY:
Marlene McGaffic, McMurray

Chicken, Black Bean, Corn & Tomato Salad

DIRECTIONS

To poach chicken, flatten breasts slightly and arrange in a single layer in saucepan or skillet. Pour cold water to cover; slowly bring water to a simmer over low heat. Once simmering, turn chicken over, cover pan and remove from heat. Let stand 15 to 20 minutes until no longer pink on inside. Transfer to a plate. Cover with plastic wrap and refrigerate until ready to use.

Tear chicken into shreds with fingers. Combine chicken with black beans, tomato and corn in a salad bowl. Heat oil in a small skillet over medium heat; add garlic and sauté until just beginning to color (about 30 seconds). Add oregano and cumin; stir until fragrant, about 10 seconds. Remove from heat. Add vinegar and salt and pour mixture over salad. Add scallions and cilantro or parsley and toss to combine.

NOTE

This salad is versatile. It may be made 8 hours ahead and stored, covered, in the refrigerator until ready to serve. For variation, add sliced onions or black olives.

INGREDIENTS

3/4 pound boneless, skinless chicken breast, trimmed and poached

1 (15-ounce) can black beans, drained and rinsed

1 large tomato or several cherry tomatoes

1/2 cup frozen corn

1 tablespoon olive oil

1 clove garlic, finely chopped

2 teaspoons oregano

1 1/2 teaspoon ground cumin

2 tablespoons apple cider vinegar

1/2 teaspoon salt

1/2 cup chopped scallions (optional)

1/4 cup chopped, fresh cilantro or parsley

SUBMITTED BY:
JoAnn Hilliard, East Liverpool

America's
HOME COOKING

Curried Fruit & Nut Salad

DIRECTIONS

Combine lettuce, spinach, orange sections, grapes and nuts in salad bowl. In a screw-top jar, combine oil, vinegar, garlic, brown sugar, curry powder, green onion and soy sauce. Immediately before serving, toss salad with some, but not all, of the dressing. Garnish with avocado. Remaining dressing can be passed with salad. Serves 8.

INGREDIENTS

1 head red leaf or romaine lettuce, torn

1 cup torn fresh spinach

1 (11-ounce) can mandarin oranges, chilled and drained

1 cup seedless grapes

1/2 cup slivered almonds or chopped walnuts

1/2 cup olive oil

1/3 cup white wine vinegar

1 clove garlic, minced

2 tablespoons packed brown sugar

1 tablespoon curry powder

2 tablespoons minced green onion

1 teaspoon soy sauce

1 avocado, peeled, seeded and sliced, for garnishing

SUBMITTED BY:
Ruth Sacco, Squirrel Hill

Easter Salad

DIRECTIONS

Beat cream cheese with mixer. Add next 3 ingredients by hand. Whip cream and fold into mixture. Refrigerate overnight.

NOTE

If mixture seems too thin, add a few more marshmallows before folding in whip cream.

INGREDIENTS

1 (8-ounce) package cream cheese, softened

1 (16-ounce) can crushed pineapple, drained

1/2 (10-ounce) jar maraschino cherries, chopped

1/2 (10 1/2-ounce) bag miniature marshmallows

1 (1/2-pint) carton whipping cream

SUBMITTED BY:
Dolores Osman, Pittsburgh

America's
HOME COOKING

Easy Chicken Rivel Soup

DIRECTIONS

Bring water to a boil and add the bouillon cubes. Stir over low heat until dissolved. (Bring mixture back to boiling for the next step.) Mix the egg and flour together (mixture will be dry and crumbly) and slowly drizzle into the boiling water and bring to low boil again. At that time, the rivels will have risen to the top. Still over low heat, add can of creamed corn and 2 to 3 cups milk (depending on the thickness desired). Heat thoroughly, but do not boil. Add salt and pepper to taste.

INGREDIENTS

5 cups water

4 chicken bouillon cubes

1 egg

1 cup flour

1 (14 1/2-ounce) can creamed corn

2 to 3 cups milk

Salt and pepper, to taste

SUBMITTED BY:
Hilary Zubritzky, McKees Rocks

39

French Chicken Salad

DIRECTIONS

Cook shells as directed and drain well. Combine all ingredients, except salad dressing and salt and pepper. Cover and refrigerate overnight. When ready to serve, add salad dressing and salt and pepper, to taste. Combine well.

NOTE

Salad can be served over a bed of chopped lettuce.

INGREDIENTS

4 cups (approximately 1 pound) medium pasta shells

3 or 4 chicken breasts, cooked and cubed

1 cup finely diced celery

1/2 medium onion, finely diced

1/2 cup finely diced green pepper (optional)

1 (12-ounce) jar French dressing

4 hard-boiled eggs, diced

Salad dressing, to taste

Salt and pepper, to taste

Lettuce, chopped, for serving (optional)

SUBMITTED BY:
Andrea Gambrel, Poland

America's
HOME COOKING

Grandma Perskey's Cabbage Soup

DIRECTIONS

In a large soup pot, sauté onion, celery and carrot in oil until tender, but not brown. Add water, cabbage and undrained tomatoes. Bring to a boil; lower heat and simmer for 30 minutes. Add lemon juice, brown sugar, salt and pepper. If using, add sliced meat. Simmer 15 minutes longer. Serves 4.

INGREDIENTS

2 tablespoons oil

1 onion, chopped

2 celery stalks, chopped

1 large carrot, chopped or shredded

6 cups water

1 small head cabbage, shredded coarsely

2 cups canned tomatoes, undrained

2 tablespoons lemon juice

1/4 cup brown sugar

2 teaspoons salt

Pepper, to taste

Sliced hot dogs, smoked sausage or kielbasa (optional)

SUBMITTED BY:
Susan Cohen, Pittsburgh

Grandma's French Dressing

DIRECTIONS

Combine all ingredients in a blender or food processor; mix until smooth.

INGREDIENTS

1 (10 3/4-ounce) can tomato soup

1 1/2 cups corn oil

1 cup sugar

1 tablespoon salt

1 teaspoon pepper

1 tablespoon prepared mustard

1 small onion, chopped

2 small, fresh garlic cloves, chopped

1/3 teaspoon paprika

3/4 cup cider vinegar

SUBMITTED BY:
Ruth Mason, Aliquippa

America's
HOME COOKING

Grandma's Vegetable Soup

DIRECTIONS

Place short ribs in large soup pot. Add water, tomatoes, vegetable juice, onions, dried parsley, bouillon, seasonings, salt, pepper, worcestershire sauce and bay leaves. Bring to a boil over high heat. Cover the pot, reduce heat to simmer the liquid and cook for 2 hours or until the meat is very tender. When done, remove meat from pot and cut, discarding fat and bones. Return meat to the pot. Add vegetables and macaroni; return to a boil. Simmer for 45 minutes.

NOTE

To remove fat from the surface of the soup, add a few ice cubes and the fat will cling to the cubes.

INGREDIENTS

3 pounds beef short ribs

4 quarts cold water

1 (28-ounce) can tomatoes

28 ounces vegetable juice

2 cups onion

3 tablespoons dried parsley

2 tablespoons beef bouillon granules

2 tablespoons chicken bouillon granules

1 tablespoon dried Italian seasoning

1 tablespoon salt

1 tablespoon pepper

1 tablespoon worcestershire sauce

2 bay leaves

1 cup chopped carrots

1 cup chopped celery

1 cup chopped fresh or frozen green beans

1 cup corn kernels

1 cup potatoes or any favorite vegetable

1 cup elbow macaroni

SUBMITTED BY:
Ruth Cassidy

America's
HOME COOKING

43

Green Bean and Potato Soup

DIRECTIONS

Cover green beans and potatoes with water and cook until potatoes are soft. Do not drain. Mix milk, egg and flour in mixing bowl; strain if lumpy. Add to cooked beans and potatoes. Cook until thick, stirring occasionally. Serve.

VARIATION

This recipe is especially good with fresh green beans from the garden, but frozen beans—not canned—can be used. Chicken broth can be substituted for the water or chicken bouillon can be added to the water. Adjust the amounts of beans or potatoes according to preference.

INGREDIENTS

1 pound fresh green beans, cut into 1-inch pieces

3 cups potatoes, cut into 1/2-inch pieces

Water

1 quart milk

1 egg

1/2 to 3/4 cup flour

Salt and pepper, to taste

SUBMITTED BY:
Adrienne Adams, Sarver

America's
HOME COOKING

Italian Macaroni Salad

DIRECTIONS

Cook macaroni; cool. Add prepared
ingredients and dressing. Refrigerate.

INGREDIENTS

1 pound elbow macaroni

1/4 pound provolone cheese,
diced

1/4 pound salami, diced

1/4 pound pepperoni, diced

3 pieces celery, chopped

1 (2 1/4-ounce) can black
pitted olives, sliced

1 small onion, chopped

2 green peppers, chopped

3 tomatoes, diced (optional)

DRESSING:

1 1/2 teaspoons salt

1 teaspoon black pepper

3/4 cup oil

1/2 cup vinegar

1 teaspoon oregano

SUBMITTED BY:
Joyce Russman, Lowellville

Langostino Corn Chowder

DIRECTIONS

Place bacon in large pot and cook over low heat, stirring constantly, for about 6 minutes. Add butter. Keep heat low and add onion. Cook until soft, about 8 minutes. Stir in flour and cook for about 1 minute. Add broth, bay leaves, paprika, thyme and potatoes. Cook for about 15 to 20 minutes. Add half & half or cream, corn, peppers and green onions or scallions and simmer for about 10 minutes. Add salt and pepper, to taste. Add langoustines and parsley and warm through before serving. Serve hot. Serves 8.

INGREDIENTS

1/4 pound bacon, finely diced

1 tablespoon butter

2 cups diced onion

2 tablespoons flour

4 cups chicken broth

2 bay leaves

1 teaspoon regular paprika

1 teaspoon thyme

2 potatoes, peeled and diced

1 cup half & half or light cream

2 (8-ounce) cans crisp corn or 2 to 3 cups fresh corn off the cob

1 red, yellow or orange bell pepper, diced

4 green onions or scallions, thinly sliced

Salt and freshly cracked pepper, to taste

1 to 1 1/2 pounds of langoustines

1/4 cup flat-leaf parsley, coarsely chopped (optional)

SUBMITTED BY:
Roberta Bauer, Wexford

America's
HOME COOKING

Lemon Glazed Fruit Salad

DIRECTIONS

Place pineapple, fruit cocktail, oranges, peaches or pears, lemon juice and instant pudding in a bowl and mix until well coated. Refrigerate for at least 4 hours, preferably overnight. Just before serving, slice and add 2 large, firm bananas and 1 pint of fresh strawberries.

VARIATION

If strawberries are not in season, use maraschino cherries cut in half. For a different twist, add finely sliced fresh mint.

INGREDIENTS

1 (20-ounce) can pineapple chunks in natural juice, undrained

1 (16-ounce) can of fruit cocktail in natural juice, drain 1/2 of the liquid and reserve remaining juice and fruit

1 (15-ounce) can of mandarin oranges, completely drained

1 (16-ounce) can of peach or pear slices in natural juice, coarsely chopped; drain 1/2 of the liquid and reserve remaining juice and fruit

2 tablespoons lemon juice

1 (3-ounce) box instant lemon pudding

2 large bananas, sliced

1 pint fresh strawberries and maraschino cherries, sliced

SUBMITTED BY:
Denean Y. Ross, Pittsburgh

America's
HOME COOKING

Lime Cheese Salad

DIRECTIONS

Drain pineapple. Dissolve gelatin in 2 cups boiling water and stir until dissolved. Add juice from pineapple and enough cold water to make 2 cups. Put in refrigerator until partially set. Add cream cheese and beat with mixer until cheese is in small chunks. Add pineapple, celery and nuts. Mix until blended and return to refrigerator to set. Serve on lettuce with a dollop of salad dressing or with butter crackers.

INGREDIENTS

1 (20-ounce) can crushed pineapple

1 (6-ounce) box lime gelatin

1 (8-ounce) package cream cheese, softened to room temperature

Celery, chopped

Nuts, chopped

Lettuce, for serving

Salad dressing, for serving

Butter crackers, for serving

SUBMITTED BY:
Ruth Logsdon, Dillonvale

America's
HOME COOKING

Old-Fashioned Potato Salad

DIRECTIONS

Stir all ingredients together to mix, cover and chill several hours before serving. Serve as is or in crisp lettuce cups.

VARIATION

For herbed potato salad, prepare recipe as directed but add 2 tablespoons minced fresh dill or 1/2 teaspoon dill weed and 1/2 teaspoon minced fresh marjoram or 1/4 teaspoon dried marjoram.

INGREDIENTS

6 medium boiled potatoes, chilled, peeled and cubed

4 hard-boiled eggs, chilled, peeled and diced

1/2 medium sweet green pepper, cored, seeded and minced

1 medium yellow onion, peeled and minced

2 stalks celery, diced

1 cup mayonnaise

1/4 cup sweet pickle relish

1 1/2 teaspoons salt

1/8 teaspoon pepper

Crisp lettuce cups, for serving (optional)

SUBMITTED BY:
Deborah Hilty, Harrison City

Special Spinach Salad

DIRECTIONS

Combine vinegar, oil, sugar, salt, pepper, onion, dry mustard and cottage cheese. Mix well to blend ingredients. Pour over prepared spinach and toss. Top with bacon.

INGREDIENTS

3 tablespoons vinegar

1/2 cup oil

2 tablespoons sugar

1/2 teaspoon salt

1/2 teaspoon pepper

1 teaspoon onion, minced

1/2 teaspoon dry mustard

3/4 cup cottage cheese

1 (10-ounce) bag fresh spinach, stems removed, cleaned and drained

6 to 10 slices cooked bacon, crumbled

SUBMITTED BY:
Debbie Chuba, Johnstown

Tortellini Soup

DIRECTIONS

In a large soup pot, sauté carrots, celery, onion and garlic in olive oil for 5 minutes. Add chicken stock and bring to a boil. Reduce heat; add stewed tomatoes and basil. Simmer for 20 minutes or until vegetables are tender. Add prepared cheese tortellini and fresh spinach. Simmer 5 more minutes. Ladle into bowls and garnish with parmesan cheese. Serve with warm crusty Italian bread and butter.

VARIATION

Add any favorite vegetables to this soup— broccoli, cauliflower, sweet red or green peppers, green beans and zucchini, among others. Substitute beef tortellini and beef stock for a heartier version.

INGREDIENTS

3 tablespoons olive oil

3 to 4 carrots, chopped

3 to 4 celery stalks, chopped

1 medium onion, chopped

3 cloves garlic, peeled and chopped

1 (50-ounce) can chicken or vegetable stock

1 (14 1/2-ounce) can stewed tomatoes, chopped

Fresh basil leaves, chopped, or 1 to 2 teaspoons dried basil

1 (8-ounce) package frozen cheese tortellini, cooked

1 handful fresh spinach, chopped

1/4 cup parmesan cheese, grated

Crusty Italian bread and butter, for serving

SUBMITTED BY:
Cecil Corson

Tuscan Sausage Soup

DIRECTIONS

Fry sausage until crumbly, remove from pot and drain all but 2 tablespoons fat. Cook onions in the fat until caramelized, add mushrooms and cook 2 to 3 minutes, then add rice. Keep stirring for another 1 to 2 minutes then add garlic, chicken stock, water, herbs and tomatoes. Simmer for 30 minutes and serve.

INGREDIENTS

1 pound Italian sweet sausage

1 medium-size cooking onion

3/4 cup sliced mushrooms

1/4 cup arborio rice

2 cloves garlic

1 (48-ounce) can chicken stock

2 cups water

Sage, to taste

Rosemary, to taste

1 (28-ounce) can plum tomatoes, cut into chunks

SUBMITTED BY:
Cay Welch, Blairsville

Vegetable Beef Soup

DIRECTIONS

Heat a small amount of oil in a skillet. Add
chopped onions and celery and sauté until
tender. Cut chuck roast into small pieces. In
same skillet, brown meat evenly on at least 2
sides. Add both the meat and sautéed
vegetables to a slow cooker. Deglaze pan with
water. Add beef broth and tomatoes to the slow
cooker. Peel and dice potatoes and add to slow
cooker with salt and pepper, bay leaves,
parsley and barley. Add enough water to cover.
Do not add vegetables. At this point, the soup
can be refrigerated overnight. The next day,
cook on high for 8 to 10 hours. Just before
serving, add the vegetables.

VARIATION

If desired, soup can be eaten on the same
day it's prepared by cooking the meat for 45
minutes in water and broth with the onion,
barley, bay leaf, parsley and celery. Add the
potatoes and cook 15 minutes more; then add
the vegetables before serving.

INGREDIENTS

Oil

1 cup chopped onions

1 cup chopped celery

3 to 4 pounds chuck roast

1 (15-ounce) can beef broth

1 (15-ounce) can tomatoes

4 potatoes, peeled and diced

Salt and pepper, to taste

Bay leaves

Parsley, to taste

1/4 cup medium barley

1 (10-ounce) box frozen green beans

1 (10-ounce) box frozen peas and carrots

SUBMITTED BY:
Virginia Jakub, Nottingham Township

America's
HOME COOKING

Veggie Potato Salad

DIRECTIONS

Toss potatoes and vegetables. Blend Italian salad dressing and seasonings. Add to potato mixture and toss to coat. Cover and refrigerate for 1 hour.

INGREDIENTS

1 pound small red potatoes, cooked and cubed

1 1/2 cups chopped fresh broccoli

1/2 cup sliced celery

1/4 cup chopped red onion

1/4 cup sliced radishes

1/4 cup chopped green pepper

1/3 cup fat-free Italian salad dressing

1/4 teaspoon salt

1/4 teaspoon dill weed

SUBMITTED BY:
Betty Pandullo, Blairsville

America's
HOME COOKING

America's
HOME COOKING
FAMILY FAVORITES
Pasta and Potatoes

Angelic Sweet Potatoes

DIRECTIONS

Preheat oven to 350 degrees. Combine all ingredients and mix well. Put in a 2-quart casserole pan. Cover with topping.

To form topping, combine all ingredients and mix well. The mixture will be crumbly. Sprinkle on top of potato mixture. Bake for 25 to 30 minutes.

NOTE

If serving a large crowd, recipe can be doubled or tripled.

INGREDIENTS

3 cups cooked sweet potatoes, mashed

1 cup sugar, preferably a combination of 1/2 cup granulated sugar and 1/2 cup brown sugar

1/2 cup melted butter

1 egg

1/3 cup milk

1 teaspoon vanilla

TOPPING:

1/2 cup brown sugar

1/4 cup flour

2 1/2 tablespoons melted butter

1/2 cup chopped pecans or walnuts (optional)

SUBMITTED BY:
Heidi and Monica Narr, Crafton

Artichoke Stuffed Manicotti

DIRECTIONS

Boil manicotti shells according to package directions. Drain in a colander, rinsing under cold water. Preheat oven to 375 degrees. Spray a 9x13-inch baking dish with nonstick spray. Combine the artichoke hearts, ricotta, parmesan, scallions or onion, salt and pepper in a food processor until fairly smooth. Using a pastry bag (with no tip) or small spoon, fill each manicotti tube with about 3 tablespoons of the artichoke mixture. Spread 1 cup of the marinara sauce in the bottom of the baking dish. Place each manicotti in the sauce. Sprinkle with mozzarella and parmesan. Cover with waxed paper and foil. Bake for 45 minutes or until bubbly. Remove cover and continue baking until cheese bubbles, about 10 minutes longer.

NOTE

As prepared, 2 shells contain 228 calories. Meat sauce may be substituted for the low-fat marinara sauce, but the recipe will contain more fat and calories

SUBMITTED BY:
Rosemarie Weleski, Natrona Heights

INGREDIENTS

1 (8-ounce) box manicotti shells, about 12 shells

2 (14 1/2-ounces) cans quartered artichokes in water, drained

1 (8-ounce) container of part-skim ricotta

1/3 cup freshly grated parmesan cheese

1/4 cup chopped green scallions or yellow onion

1/4 teaspoon salt

1/4 teaspoon pepper

2 cups marinara sauce, preferably fat-free sauce

1/2 cup shredded part-skim mozzarella cheese, shredded

Parmesan cheese, for topping (optional)

Au Gratin Potatoes

DIRECTIONS

Preheat oven to 350 degrees. Boil potatoes in salted water for 10 minutes. Drain. Melt butter and blend in flour, salt and pepper. Add milk; cook until thick. Stir in pimentos, onions, cheese, hot pepper sauce and potatoes. Pour into 2-quart buttered casserole. Combine bread-crumbs and melted butter; sprinkle on top of potatoes. Bake for 30 minutes.

INGREDIENTS

6 medium potatoes, peeled and diced

1/4 cup butter

1/3 cup flour

1 teaspoon salt

1/8 teaspoon pepper

2 cups milk

2 tablespoons pimentos, chopped

4 green onions, thinly sliced

6 ounces sharp cheddar cheese, grated

2 drops hot pepper sauce

1/2 cup breadcrumbs

2 tablespoons butter, melted

SUBMITTED BY:
Alyson Sprague, Sewickley

America's
HOME COOKING

Aunt Helen's Baked Spaghetti

Directions

Preheat oven to 325 degrees. Mix first 4 ingredients. Pour thin layer of sauce on the bottom of a 2-quart casserole; add hot, cooked pasta. Pour remaining tomato mixture over pasta and stir to mix. Cover with foil and bake for 30 to 40 minutes. Remove foil during last 10 minutes of cooking time.

Variation

Brown pork chops and lay them on top of spaghetti mixture; bake as directed.

Ingredients

2 (16-ounce) cans stewed tomatoes, finely crushed

1/3 to 1/2 cup sugar

1 small green pepper, finely chopped

1/2 pound pasteurized process cheese, cubed

3/4 pound angel hair pasta, cooked al dente

Submitted by:
Dana Stainbrook, Washington

61

Baked Perciatelli

DIRECTIONS

Preheat oven to 350 degrees. (If desired, prepare homemade spaghetti sauce.) Place enough spaghetti sauce in a 9-inch square pan to cover bottom. Cook perciatelli until al dente. Drain and rinse pasta. Place half of the pasta on top of the sauce in pan. Add a layer of cooked ground meat. Sprinkle with parmesan cheese and a layer of sauce. Top with layer of pasta. Beat remaining parmesan cheese into eggs. Pour beaten eggs over top of pasta, using a fork to insure eggs incorporate with pasta. Bake for 30 to 40 minutes. (Do not overbake as it will dry the pasta.) Remove dish from oven and let sit for another 10 minutes; cut into squares. Serve with extra sauce.

NOTE

Recipe can be doubled to fit a 9x13-inch pan.

INGREDIENTS

Spaghetti sauce, homemade or canned

1 pound perciatelli pasta

1/2 pound lean ground meat, fried and drained

1/2 cup parmesan cheese

4 eggs, beaten

SUBMITTED BY:
Rita DiFrancesco, O'Hara Township

America's HOME COOKING

Bobalki
(Slovak Christmas Eve Dish)

DIRECTIONS

Bring milk to scalding point. Remove from heat; add margarine, sugar and salt. Set aside to cool. In a small bowl, add yeast to warm water. Add a teaspoon of sugar to quickly activate the yeast. Combine milk mixture, eggs, yeast and 2/3 of the flour. Beat until smooth. Gradually add remaining flour. Turn onto floured board and knead until smooth and elastic. Place in greased bowl to rise for 1 hour.

On floured board, divide dough into 4 or 5 parts. Make each ball of dough into a rope about 1 inch thick; cut into 3/4-inch pieces. Place on greased baking sheets; allowing space between bobalki. Let rise for 1 hour. Heat oven to 350 degrees; bake for 10 to 15 minutes or until golden. Remove from pan; cool. When ready to serve, mix honey, poppy seed and browned butter. Place bobalki into a colander and pour scalding water over them. Immediately put bobalki into serving bowl and pour the dressing over them and serve.

NOTE

Bobalki can be made weeks ahead of time; store them in plastic bags or closed containers after baking and cooling. When ready to serve, finish recipe by scalding and dressing bobalki.

SUBMITTED BY:
Marge Samek, Monroeville

INGREDIENTS

2 cups milk

1/2 cup margarine

1 cup sugar

2 teaspoons salt

1 packet yeast

1 cup warm, not hot, water

1 teaspoon sugar

2 eggs

8 cups flour

DRESSING:

1 cup (2 sticks) butter, browned

24 ounces honey

1 1/2 pounds poppy seed

America's
HOME COOKING

Brother-in-Law Rigatoni Sosso

DIRECTIONS

Heat olive oil and butter on medium heat; add onion, stirring for 2 minutes. Add celery, carrot and garlic; stir for 2 more minutes to coat. Season with salt and pepper, to taste. Add both sausages; crumble until brown. Add milk, turn down heat to medium or low and let simmer gently uncovered until milk has evaporated. Add wine and simmer until it evaporates. Add tomatoes, cover pot and bring to a boil. Reduce heat again to the lowest setting. Cook for 2 hours with pot lid slightly ajar, stirring occasionally and adding reserved tomato juice as needed. Serve over rigatoni with a generous portion of grated cheese.

INGREDIENTS

2 tablespoons olive oil

2 tablespoons butter

1/2 cup chopped onion

1/2 cup chopped celery

1/2 cup chopped carrot

4 cloves garlic, minced

Salt, to taste

Black pepper, to taste

1/2 pound bulk hot sausage

1/2 pound bulk sweet sausage

1 cup milk, at room temperature

1 cup dry white wine

1 (14 1/2-ounce) can diced tomatoes, reserving juice

1 pound rigatoni, cooked, for serving

Parmesan cheese, freshly grated, for serving

SUBMITTED BY:
Larry Broderick, Gibsonia

America's
HOME COOKING

Butternut Squash Gnocchi with Sage

DIRECTIONS

Boil squash in microwave for about 12 minutes or until cooked. Drain and put through ricer. Drain squash on paper towels until only 3/4 cup of vegetable remains. Scoop out pulp from hot baked potatoes and put through ricer; cool on a cookie sheet. In a large bowl, mix eggs and add squash, potatoes, parmesan cheese, nutmeg and salt. Stir in 3/4 cup flour. Knead in about 1/4 to 1/2 cup flour. Divide dough into 4 pieces. Roll out gnocchi; boil until pasta floats. Drain and stir into sauce.

To prepare sage sauce, melt butter in a small pan and sauté sage leaves for 1 or 2 minutes. Pour over gnocchi and sprinkle with grated cheese and fresh pepper.

NOTE

Gnocchi can be frozen and stored before cooking.

INGREDIENTS

1 small butternut squash, peeled and cut into cubes

2 large baking potatoes, baked

2 large eggs

1/4 cup parmesan cheese

Fresh nutmeg, to taste

1 1/4 teaspoons salt

1 1/2 cups flour

SAGE SAUCE:

2 tablespoons (1/4 stick) butter

4 sage leaves

1/4 cup parmesan cheese, grated

Fresh pepper

SUBMITTED BY:
Barbara Knezovich, McKeesport

Donna's Italian Pasta Stew

DIRECTIONS

In a large pan, combine broth, celery, carrots and onions. Bring to a boil, reduce heat, cover and simmer for 5 minutes or until vegetables are tender crisp. Stir in vegetable juice, tomatoes, tomato paste, oregano and black pepper. Cover and simmer 30 minutes. Meanwhile, in a skillet, brown sausage, green pepper and garlic until no longer pink. Drain. Add beans and meat to broth and vegetables. Cover and simmer for 45 minutes. Add pasta and cook for about 5 minutes or until pasta is heated through. Garnish with parmesan cheese. Serves 8.

INGREDIENTS

1 1/2 cups beef broth

2 celery stalks, chopped

2 large carrots, sliced 1/4 inch thick

1 medium onion, chopped

1 (46-ounce) can vegetable juice

1 (14 1/2-ounces) can Italian diced tomatoes, undrained

2 (6-ounce) cans Italian tomato paste

1 tablespoon dried oregano

1 1/2 teaspoons black pepper

3/4 pounds mild or hot Italian sausage

1/2 green pepper, chopped

2 cloves garlic, minced

3/4 cups canned kidney beans, rinsed and drained

3/4 cups canned northern beans, rinsed and drained

1 cup medium pasta shells, cooked

Parmesan cheese, shredded

Crushed red pepper flakes (optional)

Chopped parsley (optional)

SUBMITTED BY:
Donna Sunderlin, DuBois

Haluski Drop Dumplings (Grated Potatoes)

DIRECTIONS

Combine chopped cabbage, salt, 3 tablespoons shortening and 1/2 of the chopped onions in a skillet. Fry slowly for about 20 minutes until vegetables are tender. Sauté remaining onions in 2 tablespoons margarine; set aside.

To make dumplings, add salt, egg and flour to grated potatoes and mix well. Dough should not be too thin; use more or less flour depending on the size of the potatoes. Place dough on a plate; drop dough into boiling water a teaspoon of batter at a time. Boil about 15 minutes, stirring to prevent scorching. Drain in colander. Combine dumplings and sautéed cabbage; mix well. Drizzle sautéed onion over top to serve.

INGREDIENTS

1 (2-pound) head cabbage, chopped

1 teaspoon salt

3 tablespoons shortening or margarine

2 small onions, chopped and divided

2 tablespoons shortening or margarine

DUMPLINGS:

1 teaspoon salt

1 egg

3 cups flour

2 large potatoes, grated

SUBMITTED BY:
Marge Samek, Monroeville

67

Nonna's Broccoli and Pasta

DIRECTIONS

Cook bacon in pan. Remove and crumble bacon; reserve grease. Steam broccoli until tender, but not mushy, in salted water. Remove broccoli and cut into bite-size pieces. Cook pasta according to package directions. Mix pasta, broccoli and crumbled bacon. Add bacon grease to pasta by the spoonful to coat; stir well.

INGREDIENTS

1 pound bacon

1 pound fresh broccoli

1 pound small pasta shells

SUBMITTED BY:
Nina Ward, Washington

America's
HOME COOKING

Noodle Bake

DIRECTIONS

Preheat oven to 350 degrees. Boil noodles, drain and coat with butter. Cream together cream cheese, sugar and eggs. Add to noodles along with pineapple and juices and milk. Mix it all together and pour into a 13x9-inch pan. To make topping, mix all ingredients together. Then, sprinkle topping on noodles. Bake for 45 minutes then turn off heat but leave noodle bake in oven for an additional 30 minutes.

INGREDIENTS

1 (8-ounce) package medium noodles

6 tablespoons (3/4 stick) butter

1 (8-ounce) package cream cheese

1/2 cup sugar

3 eggs

1 (20-ounce) can crushed pineapple with juice

1/4 cup milk

TOPPING:

1 1/4 cup crushed corn flakes

4 or 6 tablespoons (1/2 or 3/4 stick) margarine

1/4 cup sugar

1 teaspoon cinnamon

SUBMITTED BY:
Patty Roydes, Clinton Township

Penne Alla Noci

DIRECTIONS

Put olive oil, garlic and walnuts or hazelnuts into a pan and add sun-dried tomatoes and red chili flakes (flakes will increase spiciness). Cook slightly; add breadcrumbs and toss. Turn off heat and mix in chopped fresh parsley. Add pasta and 1/4 cup pasta water and toss to coat. Add cheese, basil, and salt and pepper; toss again. Serve immediately or chill and serve as pasta salad.

INGREDIENTS

1/4 cup olive oil

2 cloves of garlic, sliced thin

1/4 cup chopped walnuts or hazelnuts

6 sun-dried tomato halves in oil, chopped

Red chili flakes, to taste (optional)

4 tablespoons of toasted breadcrumbs

1/4 cup chopped fresh parsley

1 (1-pound) box penne, cooked in salt water and drained

1/4 cup pasta water

1/4 cup parmesan cheese

1/2 teaspoon dried basil

Salt and pepper, to taste

SUBMITTED BY:
Nina Mule Lyons, Pittsburgh

Perogie Casserole

DIRECTIONS

Preheat oven to 350 degrees. Cook noodles according to package directions. Sauté onion in butter. Mash potatoes with milk and 1/4 of the cheese. In a 9x13-inch pan, layer the onions and butter, noodles and remaining cheese. Repeat until all ingredients are used. Bake, covered, for 15 minutes. Uncover and bake for an additional 5 minutes.

INGREDIENTS

1 (12-ounce) package bow tie noodles

1/2 pound butter

1 large onion

5 to 6 medium potatoes

Milk

1 (8-ounce) package pasteurized process cheese

SUBMITTED BY:
Patty Roydes, Clinton Township

Potato Balls

DIRECTIONS

Mix all ingredients together. Roll into golf ball-size balls. Drop them into boiling, salted water and cook until the balls rise to the surface. Drain and add tomato sauce. Serve topped with grated cheese.

INGREDIENTS

4 cups mashed potatoes

4 cups bread crumbs

1 cup grated parmesan cheese

1/2 pound ricotta cheese

2 tablespoons shortening

4 eggs

3 cups flour

Tomato sauce, for serving

Grated cheese, for serving

SUBMITTED BY:
Catherine Monte Carlo, Monongahela

America's
HOME COOKING

Potato Dumplings and Kraut

DIRECTIONS

Brown diced onion in 1 stick of melted butter until golden. Add kraut and cook over medium-low heat for approximately 30 minutes. Peel potatoes, cut into medium chunks and place in a blender. Fill blender with just enough water to cover potatoes. Process potatoes on high until all chunks are gone and mixture is smooth. Strain potatoes through a mesh strainer to remove all water. Put potatoes into a bowl; add egg, salt and half of the flour. Mix well and add almost or all of the remaining flour. Place dough onto a plate and, with a spoon, drop small portions into boiling salted water. Cook until dumplings rise to the top. Scoop out with slotted spoon and drop into the kraut mixture. Add last stick of butter and let dumplings simmer until all butter has melted. Add salt and pepper as needed.

INGREDIENTS

KRAUT:

1 large sweet onion, diced

1 cup (2 sticks) butter

1 (16-ounce) bag sauerkraut

DUMPLINGS:

2 medium potatoes

1 egg

1 teaspoon salt

2 cups flour

Salt and pepper, to taste

SUBMITTED BY:
Susie Dorich, McKeesport

Potato Latkes

DIRECTIONS

Peel and cube potatoes. Place in food processor with ice water and lemon juice. Process with metal blade until finely grated. Drain well in a fine strainer. Combine remaining ingredients in a large bowl. Add grated potatoes and mix gently, but well. Heat 1/4 inch of vegetable oil or solid shortening in a large skillet. Drop batter by heaping table-spoonfuls to form 2 1/2-inch pancakes. Fry over medium heat for 1 1/2 to 2 minutes on each side or until browned; drain well on paper towels. Keep warm in a 200-degree oven until all pancakes are fried. Serve with honeyed applesauce (see page 197). Makes about 16 pancakes.

INGREDIENTS

6 large red-skinned potatoes

2 tablespoons ice water

1 tablespoon lemon juice

3 eggs

1/3 cup matzo meal

1/4 cup chopped green onion

1/4 teaspoon baking powder

1 teaspoon salt

1/4 teaspoon pepper

Vegetable oil or shortening

SUBMITTED BY:
Susan Cohen, Pittsburgh

America's
HOME COOKING

Rice Pilaf

DIRECTIONS

Preheat oven to 350 degrees. Sauté onions
and pepper in butter. In a 2-quart casserole, mix
together remaining ingredients. Stir in the
onions, pepper and butter. Bake, uncovered, for
1 hour and 15 minutes.

INGREDIENTS

1 onion, diced

1 green pepper, diced

1/2 cup (1 stick) butter

1 cup converted rice

1 (4-ounce) can mushrooms

1 (14 1/2-ounce) can
beef broth

1 (10 3/4-ounce) can French
onion soup

SUBMITTED BY:
Ellen Matthews, Greensburg

Ricotta Gnocchi

DIRECTIONS

Combine ricotta, salt and egg in mixer. With a dough hook, add enough flour so the dough forms a ball. Continue mixing with hook for 1 to 2 minutes to knead. If not using dough hook, turn ball onto lightly floured board and knead until dough is smooth, about 5 minutes. Divide dough into small handfuls and roll into long finger-sized rolls, about 1/2 to 1 inch in diameter. Cut each roll into 1-inch pieces. With index finger, press each piece of dough in the center while gently, but firmly, rolling down a fork until the dough curls around the fork tines. If gnocchi are very thick, turn the piece of dough and curl the other side as well. Let stand for 10 to 15 minutes on flour-dusted cookie sheets. To cook, drop into rapidly boiling salted water, being careful to avoid crowding the pot. Boil until tender, about 5 minutes, or until gnocchi float to the surface of the water. Drain well and add spaghetti sauce and plenty of grated parmesan cheese. Makes 220 to 225 gnocchi, which serves 10 to 12 people.

INGREDIENTS

2 pounds ricotta cheese

1 teaspoon salt

1 egg

5 to 6 cups flour

Spaghetti sauce, for serving

Parmesan cheese, grated, for serving

NOTE

To freeze, place uncooked gnocchi on cookie sheets in freezer until frozen. Remove and place in plastic bags and store in freezer. To cook, drop frozen gnocchi into rapidly boiling water and cook as above.

SUBMITTED BY:
Marlene McGaffic, McMurray

Ricotta Sauce with Walnuts

DIRECTIONS

Place all ingredients, except pasta, into blender or food processor and blend well. Adjust consistency of sauce with milk. Cook pasta, drain and return to pot. Add sauce, toss and serve with grated parmesan.

INGREDIENTS

1/3 cup walnuts

1/3 cup olive oil

1/2 cup grated parmesan cheese

1/2 cup fresh parsley, chopped

1/2 cup ricotta

1/3 cup milk

1/4 pound butter, melted

1 large clove garlic, chopped

1 teaspoon salt

1/2 teaspoon pepper

1 pound fettuccine

Grated parmesan, for serving

SUBMITTED BY:
Suzanne Tiberio, West Leechburg

77

Rigatoni with Spinach-Ricotta Filling

DIRECTIONS

Preheat oven to 350 degrees. Cook spinach for 1 minute; drain and squeeze out extra moisture. Combine spinach, ricotta, eggs, 2/3 cup romano cheese, 2/3 cup mozzarella cheese, parsley, and salt and pepper. Set aside. Cook rigatoni for 10 minutes; drain. Combine with 2 1/2 cups spaghetti sauce. Arrange 1/2 the rigatoni in an 11x7x2-inch pan or 9-inch baking dish. Evenly spread ricotta-spinach mixture over rigatoni. Cover with remaining rigatoni and spread remaining sauce on top. Sprinkle dish with 1/3 cup mozzarella cheese and 2 tablespoons grated romano cheese. Bake for 35 to 40 minutes.

INGREDIENTS

FILLING:

1 (10-ounce) box frozen chopped spinach

2 cups ricotta cheese

3 eggs, slightly beaten

2/3 cup grated romano cheese

1 cup shredded mozzarella cheese, divided

Parsley

1 teaspoon salt

1/4 teaspoon pepper

PASTA:

8 ounces rigatoni

1 (32-ounce) jar spaghetti sauce

2 tablespoons grated romano cheese

SUBMITTED BY:
Peg Bauer, Pittsburgh

Risotto

DIRECTIONS

Make broth and, once made, remove vegetables used but leave in chicken chunks. Add onion powder and salt and pepper to broth. In a large pot, bring sauce to a boil, add beef and chicken chunks and continue cooking. Pour rice into boiling sauce, stirring sauce constantly. While stirring, add broth, one cup at a time. Allow rice to absorb each cup of broth before adding another cup. Continue this process for about 45 minutes, or until all broth is used and absorbed. (The risotto should be smooth, not soupy.) Add cheese and stir. Serves 6 to 8. Serve hot with salad, fresh Italian bread and Chianti wine.

VARIATION

To make vegetarian risotto, use vegetable broth and substitute finely diced mushrooms and chopped spinach for the meat.

A mixture of hot and sweet Italian sausage can be substituted for ground beef; brown sausage with garlic before adding to the sauce. 1/2 cup sliced mushrooms can be added with the last cup of broth.

INGREDIENTS

7 cups chicken broth with chicken chunks

Onion powder, to taste

Salt and pepper, to taste

1 quart spaghetti sauce

1/2 pound ground beef

2 cups rice

1/2 cup grated romano cheese

Italian bread, for serving

SUBMITTED BY:
Joe LoBue, Adams Ridge

America's
HOME COOKING

Scalloped Potatoes

DIRECTIONS

Preheat oven to 350 degrees. Spray large oven-proofbowl with cooking spray. Peel and slice potatoes and onions into 1/4 inch thick pieces. Slice about 1/2 of the cheese block. Layer potatoes, onions and cheese. Repeat layers, ending with cheese. Make a white sauce by melting margarine in a saucepan; stir in enough flour to make a paste. Pour in milk and continuously stir or whisk until mixture thickens. Add a pinch of salt and pepper and pour over potatoes. Bake for about 1 1/2 hours or until brown on top. Cover dish with foil during the end of the baking time to prevent excessive browning, if needed. The dish is done when potatoes are soft in the center. Allow potatoes to set for about 15 minutes before serving.

INGREDIENTS

10 all-purpose white potatoes

3 large yellow onions

1 (2-pound) package pasteurized process cheese

6 tablespoons (3/4 stick) margarine

1/2 cup flour (approximate)

1 (12-ounce) can evaporated milk

4 ounces regular milk

Salt and pepper, to taste

SUBMITTED BY:
Patricia Viszneki Martinez, Brookline

80

Scalloped Potatoes Parmesan

DIRECTIONS

Preheat oven to 350 degrees. Melt butter in saucepan and stir in cheese. Add dry ingredients and stir until smooth. Slowly mix in milk, stirring until well blended. Cook until sauce is thickened. Alternate layers of sauce and potato slices in a baking dish until filled. Dot with butter and bake for 40 minutes or until potatoes are tender.

INGREDIENTS

1/2 cup (1 stick) butter

1 cup grated parmesan cheese

2 teaspoons salt

1/4 cup flour

1/2 teaspoon paprika

1/2 teaspoon pepper

2 cups milk

6 large potatoes, sliced

SUBMITTED BY:
Gloria Bowser, Kittanning

Scrippelles (Crepes)

DIRECTIONS

Sift flour into a bowl. Make a well and add eggs. Mix with an electric mixer while adding water, a little at a time. After mixing, strain to remove the lumps. Heat a frying pan and rub with a piece of salt pork that has most of the meat cut off (leaving mostly fat); then put about 1/2 a ladle of the mixture in the frying pan. Swish it around to form a thin crepe and let cook until edges are dry; turn over and cook a little longer. Turn onto a table covered with dishtowels and let cool. Continue rubbing fry pan with the salt pork for each crepe. After all the crepes are made, mix together pecorino romano cheese and pepper. Sprinkle a little of the cheese mixture on the crepe, spread it around to cover and roll up like a cigar. Layer crepes in a big serving bowl (can be stacked). Pour hot chicken broth over the crepes and let stand for 10 minutes, so that the broth can soak through. Serve in soup bowls with more hot broth.

INGREDIENTS

3 cups flour

5 eggs

2 1/2 cups water (approximate)

Salt pork

Pecorino romano cheese

Black pepper

Chicken broth, heated

SUBMITTED BY:
Marjorie DiRisio Orlando, Connellsville

Sister Mary Francis' Potatoes

DIRECTIONS

Layer potatoes, salt and parsley. Cover with cream. Cover and refrigerate overnight. Place in cold oven (do not preheat). Bake at 350 degrees, covered, for 30 minutes. Uncover and continue to bake for 15 minutes or until top browns slightly.

INGREDIENTS

5 pounds russet potatoes, boiled, cooled and grated

Seasoned salt

Fresh parsley, chopped (optional)

3 (1/2-pint) containers whipping cream

SUBMITTED BY:
Adda Swartz, Moon Township

Spaghetti Casserole

DIRECTIONS

To make sauce, fry 2 slices of bacon in a large Dutch oven until crisp. Remove bacon; use leftover bacon grease to brown beef. Remove beef and drain. Fry remaining 2 slices of bacon, removing it when crisp. Sauté onion, celery and green pepper in bacon drippings for 3 to 4 minutes. Add beef, tomato sauce, diced tomatoes, bay leaf, thyme, cayenne pepper and salt. Chop bacon and add to sauce. Simmer 1 to 1 1/2 hours, adding water if sauce becomes too thick. (The sauce can be prepared in advance.)

Preheat oven to 350 degrees. To assemble casserole, add mushrooms, if desired, to finished sauce. Layer cooked spaghetti and sauce in a large oven-safe Dutch oven or casserole dish, stirring to incorporate. Top with cheddar cheese. Cover and bake for 30 minutes; remove cover and bake for an additional 10 minutes to allow cheese to brown. Cool slightly before serving.

INGREDIENTS

4 slices bacon, divided

1 pound ground beef

1 medium onion, chopped

2 stalks celery, chopped

1 green pepper, chopped

1 (28-ounce) can tomato sauce

1 (14-ounce) can diced tomatoes

1 bay leaf

1 sprig fresh thyme or 1 1/2 teaspoons dried thyme

Dash of cayenne pepper, to taste

1 teaspoon salt

1 (4-ounce) can mushrooms (optional)

1 (16-ounce) package spaghetti, cooked

Grated cheddar cheese (optional)

SUBMITTED BY:
Elizabeth and Nancy Speed, Franklin Park and Blawnox

America's HOME COOKING

Spaghetti Pizza

DIRECTIONS

Preheat oven to 350 degrees. Brown ground beef in a skillet. Drain and run warm water over meat to wash off grease; return to skillet. Add 1/2 cup ketchup to coat meat. Cut mushrooms into small pieces and add to mixture. Add nutmeg and garlic powder and mix well. Remove from heat and let sit. To form "crust," beat eggs, add milk and mix well. Pour over spaghetti. Mix in salt, parmesan and a dash of garlic powder. Mix in enough spaghetti sauce to coat spaghetti well, but not enough to make it sloppy. (This will vary according to type of spaghetti used.) Put pasta mixture in 9x13-inch pan, press down to compact spaghetti. Bake for 20 minutes. Remove from oven and spread meat mixture evenly over top of spaghetti. Sprinkle with mozzarella cheese to cover. Return to oven for another 20 minutes. Remove and let sit for a few minutes. Serve as is or put a spoonful of spaghetti sauce on a plate and place a serving of pizza on top.

INGREDIENTS

CRUST:

2 eggs, well beaten

1/2 cup milk

3 cups cooked spaghetti

1 teaspoon salt

1/3 cup grated parmesan cheese

Dash of garlic powder, to taste

1 cup spaghetti sauce

TOPPING:

1/2 to 1 pound ground beef

1/2 to 3/4 cup ketchup

1 (4-ounce) can mushroom

Dash of nutmeg, to taste

Dash of garlic powder, to taste

1/2 cup mozzarella cheese

SUBMITTED BY:
Judith and Burton Fleming, West Sunbury

America's
HOME COOKING

Spanish Rice

DIRECTIONS

Cook ground beef, onions and peppers in a Dutch oven. Drain off excess grease and return to pot. Add rest of ingredients and heat. Serve with crusty Italian bread and butter and a salad.

INGREDIENTS

2 pounds ground beef

1 large onion, diced

2 medium green peppers, diced

1 (6-ounce) can tomato paste

1 (46-ounce) can tomato juice

6 servings rice, prepared as directed on box

Salt and pepper, to taste

Italian bread and butter, for serving

SUBMITTED BY:
Barbara Crissman, Vandergrift

Sweet Potato Casserole

DIRECTIONS

Preheat oven to 350 degrees. To prepare casserole, combine all 5 ingredients in a mixing bowl and blend with mixer. Pour into 9x9-inch baking dish. To prepare topping, mix together all ingredients with a spoon and sprinkle onto sweet potato mixture. Bake for 30 minutes.

INGREDIENTS

CASSEROLE:

3 cups mashed sweet potatoes or unsweetened canned sweet potatoes

2 eggs

1 cup sugar

1 teaspoon vanilla

1/2 cup butter

TOPPING:

1 cup packed brown sugar

1 cup chopped pecans or walnuts

1/3 cup flour

1/3 cup soft butter

SUBMITTED BY:
Glenda Kelly

Turkey Lasagna

DIRECTIONS

Preheat oven to 350 degrees. Cook and drain noodles. Blend soups, parmesan cheese, sour cream, onion, olives, pimento and garlic salt. Stir in the turkey. Spread 1/4 of turkey mixture over the bottom of a 9x13-inch pan. Alternate layers of lasagna, turkey mixture and American cheese. End with cheese. Bake for 40 to 45 minutes. Remove and let stand for 10 minutes. Cut and serve.

INGREDIENTS

1 (8-ounce) box lasagna noodles, cooked and cooled

1 (10 1/2-ounce) can cream of mushroom soup

1 (10 1/2-ounce) can cream of chicken soup

1 cup grated parmesan cheese

1 cup sour cream

1 cup chopped onion

1 cup chopped or sliced ripe olives

1/4 cup chopped pimento

1/2 teaspoon garlic salt

2 to 3 cups diced cooked turkey

2 cups shredded American cheese

SUBMITTED BY:
Janet Shockey, Somerset

FAMILY FAVORITES

Entrees

Apricot Chicken

DIRECTIONS

Preheat oven to 350 degrees. Sprinkle the chicken with garlic powder and black pepper. In one bowl, whisk egg with soy sauce and a dash or two of water. In a second bowl, lay out the breadcrumbs. Dredge the chicken in egg mixture and then roll it in the breadcrumbs. (If egg runs out, be sure to add extra soy sauce and water to maintain the mixture's proportions.) Brown the chicken lightly in oil to add texture and ensure that the breadcrumb coating doesn't cook off. Put the chicken breasts in a baking dish and place the apricots on top of each individual piece. Deglaze the frying pan with the sherry. Add the sherry and the liquid from the apricots to the baking dish with the chicken. Bake uncovered for 30 minutes. Serve over rice. Serves 4 to 6.

INGREDIENTS

3 whole chicken breasts or 6 halves

Garlic powder, to taste

Black pepper, to taste

1 egg

2 teaspoons soy sauce

Unseasoned breadcrumbs

Oil, for sautéing

1/4 cup sherry

1 (15 1/4-ounce) can apricot halves

Rice, for serving

SUBMITTED BY:
Scott Pavelle, Ross Township

America's
HOME COOKING

Baba's Sausage Bake

DIRECTIONS

Preheat oven to 350 degrees. In an ovenproof Dutch oven, place a thin layer of cabbage then evenly arrange sausage, sweet potatoes, onion and apple. Sprinkle with salt, pepper, garlic, caraway seeds and brown sugar. Add the rest of the cabbage and drizzle with melted butter. Cover, place in oven and bake 1 1/2 to 2 hours.

INGREDIENTS

1 head red cabbage, shredded

2 pounds smoked sausage, cut into 8 equal pieces

4 sweet potatoes, quartered, with skins on

1 red onion, thinly sliced

1 sweet apple, such as Fuji or pink lady, thinly sliced

1 tablespoon salt

1/2 tablespoon black pepper

2 cloves garlic, sliced

1 tablespoon caraway seeds

2 tablespoons brown sugar

1/2 cup (1 stick) butter, melted

SUBMITTED BY:
Heidi and Monica Narr, Crafton

America's
HOME COOKING

Baccala Alla Manuella

DIRECTIONS

Soak baccala for a couple of days in cold water, changing water frequently. Preheat oven to 350 degrees. Parboil baccala for about 3 minutes. Drain water, but reserve 2 to 3 cups of liquid. Spray a 1 1/2-quart casserole with cooking spray. Alternate layers of thinly sliced white potatoes, baccala and breadcrumbs with parsley. Drizzle olive oil and parboil liquid throughout dish. Use garlic in the layering process, but stick whole cloves pierced with toothpicks to make removal easier. Top dish with a layer of breadcrumbs and parsley. Cover with lid and bake for 2 1/2 hours. Check for doneness after 2 hours (some potatoes will cook more quickly than others). Remove garlic cloves when done and serve with wilted escarole.

INGREDIENTS

1 1/2 pounds boneless white baccala

All-purpose white potatoes

Breadcrumbs

Parsley

Olive oil

Garlic cloves

Escarole, wilted, for serving

SUBMITTED BY:
Lucretia Biordi Elson, Squirrel Hill

94

Barbecued Hamburgers

DIRECTIONS

Preheat oven to 300 degrees. In a large mixing bowl, soften bread in the milk or half & half. Add ground sirloin. Finely chop garlic and 1/3 of the onion and add to mixture. Add slightly beaten egg, salt and pepper, and breadcrumbs. Form into 4 thick patties. Brown patties in a small amount of oil in heavy Dutch oven or other covered pan. Remove patties. Add tomato sauce, sliced onion and sliced green pepper to pan. Place the patties into the sauce. Cover and bake for 1 hour. Remove from oven and let sit for about 10 minutes. Serve with buttered noodles.

INGREDIENTS

1 cup Italian bread or roll pieces

1/4 cup milk or half & half

1 pound lean ground sirloin

1 garlic clove

1 medium to large onion

1 egg, slightly beaten

Salt and pepper, to taste.

1/2 cup seasoned breadcrumbs

1 (15-ounce) can seasoned tomato sauce

1 green pepper, sliced

Buttered noodles, for serving

SUBMITTED BY:
Cheryl Loesch, Allison Park

95

Barnesboro Tavern Burgers

DIRECTIONS

Preheat oven to 350 degrees. Mix the ground beef, eggs, milk, oatmeal, worcestershire sauce, bread, salt and pepper in a large mixing bowl. Form into hamburger patties and layer them in a large roaster pan. Cover the burgers with the whole and crushed tomatoes. Add water to cover the burgers. Add sliced onions and peppers and layer on top of burgers. Cover and cook for 2 hours. Makes about 20 burgers.

INGREDIENTS

4 pounds ground beef

2 eggs

1/2 cup milk

1/2 cup oatmeal

1/4 cup worcestershire sauce

5 to 6 slices bread

Salt and pepper, to taste

2 (16-ounce) cans whole tomatoes

1 (16-ounce) can crushed tomatoes

Water

4 onions, sliced

2 green peppers, sliced

SUBMITTED BY:
Richard Kutchman, Oakland

Beanless Chili

DIRECTIONS

Brown the ground sirloin. Put tomatoes in a pot and season. Add peppers to pot. Add browned meat to pot and season with chili powder and salt and pepper to taste. Sauté onions with 1 to 2 cloves garlic; then add to pot. Sauté mushrooms with 1 to 2 cloves garlic; then add to pot. Put an ample amount of chili powder on top and stir. Add an equal amount of chili powder on top of chili and cover with lid. Cook on medium heat for 30 minutes. Check for thickness and add tomato paste, a little at a time, until desired consistency is reached. Turn heat down to low.

INGREDIENTS

2 pounds ground sirloin

2 (28-ounce) cans diced tomatoes

2 bell peppers, any color, chopped

Chili powder, to taste

Salt and pepper, to taste

1 large sweet onion

4 to 6 cloves garlic

1 pound mushrooms

1 (6-ounce) can tomato paste

SUBMITTED BY:
Dan Reuter, Dorseyville

America's
HOME COOKING

97

The Big Sandwich

DIRECTIONS

Whisk together salad dressing and Italian dressing to make a marinade and set aside. Prepare all other ingredients as follows: slice the zucchini long ways into 1/4-inch-thick slices; slice onion into unseparated rings; cut the top off pepper and remove core, slice open down one side and press the pepper flat (remove all membranes); cut tomato into slices about 1/8 inch thick; and cut bread horizontally and spread with some marinade (on both sides). Alternate layers of zucchini, onion, pepper, tomato and salami with marinade. Prepare layers a day ahead and refrigerate until ready to cook. Place chicken, one piece at a time, in an open plastic bag. Pound each piece until it is half its original thickness. Place in a separate pan. Pour remaining marinade on chicken and marinate for 30 minutes. Grill vegetables until cooked through; set aside. Grill the salami and chicken till done; set aside. Grill marinated bread slices. Assemble sandwich as follows: on the bottom of bread loaf, layer the chicken, zucchini, onion, tomato, pepper and salami; top bread. Insert skewers into bread in intervals. Slice into 6 or 8 pieces.

INGREDIENTS

10 ounces salad dressing

1 (8-ounce) bottle Italian dressing

1 large zucchini

1 large Vidalia onion

2 large red peppers

2 large tomatoes

1 large loaf Italian bread

4 individual boneless, skinless chicken breasts, pounded thin

1/2 pound cooked salami

3 to 4 wooden skewers, cut in half

NOTE

Sandwich ingredients can be grilled on stove and bread can be cooked in broiler. Sandwich can be wrapped in foil and kept warm.

SUBMITTED BY:
Edwynna Roach, Russellton

98

Bourbon Baked Ham

DIRECTIONS

Preheat oven to 350 degrees. Combine the sugar and molasses in small saucepan and melt over low heat. Add the bourbon, orange juice, mustard and cloves. Mix well. Prepare the ham by removing skin and excess fat. Place in lightly greased baking pan. Make 1/2-inch cuts in a diamond pattern. Pour the glaze over the ham. Bake for 2 to 2 1/2 hours or until meat thermometer registers 140 degrees. Baste ham occasionally with glaze. When done, remove from pan. Reserve the drippings and serve with ham. Chill any left-over glaze; it can be reheated.

INGREDIENTS

1 cup light brown sugar

1/2 cup molasses

1/2 cup bourbon

1 cup orange juice

2 tablespoons dijon mustard

1 tablespoon whole cloves

1 half ham

SUBMITTED BY:
Dolores Thorp, Salineville

Braciole

DIRECTIONS

Mix breadcrumbs with cheese, spices and oil. Cut the tenderloin crosswise into 1/2-inch rounds and pound to thin, three-inch circles. Put a heaping tablespoon of filling on each cutlet. Bury 1/4 of a hard-boiled egg in the stuffing and roll up tightly, tucking in the sides. Secure the bundles with toothpicks or kitchen twine. Heat the olive oil in a skillet and brown the bundles on all sides over high heat. Place the braciole into tomato sauce and simmer for at least 1 hour until tender.

INGREDIENTS

1 cup seasoned breadcrumbs

1/2 cup grated romano cheese

1 clove garlic, minced

1/4 cup minced parsley

1/2 teaspoon oregano

1/2 teaspoon basil

Salt and pepper, to taste

2 tablespoons olive oil

1 (1-pound) pork tenderloin

4 hard-boiled eggs, cut into quarters

2 tablespoons olive oil, for frying

Tomato sauce

SUBMITTED BY:
Chris Fennimore, "QED Cooks"

Bracoli

Directions

Preheat oven to 325 degrees. Mix the stuffing ingredients until well blended. Place on the thin sandwich steak and roll up; fasten with toothpicks or string. (Stuffing should fill about 5 rolls with a generous 1/4 cup of stuffing in each roll.) Brown the rolls in a little oil in a frying pan. Make the tomato sauce (or use a favorite sauce, but it should be plain). Cover the rolls with sauce; place in casserole dish. Cover casserole and cook for 1 1/2 to 2 hours. (Meat should be very tender when it's done.) Place rolls in the refrigerator until they "set," about 1 hour, then slice into rings and serve with sauce on top. Pasta and salad may be served on the side.

2 pounds round steak, pounded very thin

STUFFING:

1/4 cup chopped parsley

1/4 cup finely chopped celery

1/4 cup finely chopped onion

1/4 pound parmesan cheese, finely cubed

1 hard-boiled egg, chopped

3 to 4 slices precooked bacon, finely chopped

4 tablespoons seasoned breadcrumbs

3 tablespoons olive oil

1 garlic clove, minced

Salt and pepper, to taste

TOMATO SAUCE:

1 onion, chopped

1 clove garlic, minced

Olive oil

1 (6-ounce can) tomato paste

3 (6-ounce) cans water

1 (32-ounce) can plum tomatoes in puree, blended

Salt and pepper, to taste

Basil, to taste

Sugar, to taste

SUBMITTED BY:
Nina Mule Lyons, Pittsburgh

Chicken Elegance

DIRECTIONS

Cover chicken breasts with cold water in large pot. Add onion and celery. Cook approximately 1 hour until chicken is tender. Cool chicken and cut into bite-sized pieces. Preheat oven to 350 degrees. Combine sour cream and soup. Add cut up chicken. Place into greased 2-quart casserole. Heat chicken broth, some cooked onion and celery (if desired) and margarine. Pour over stuffing mix. Spread stuffing mix evenly on casserole. Bake for 30 minutes. Thicken leftover broth for gravy. Serves 6.

INGREDIENTS

4 whole chicken breasts

Onion, chopped

Celery, chopped

Garlic, chopped (optional)

1 pint sour cream

1 (10 1/2-ounce) cream of chicken or cream of mushroom soup

1 cup chicken broth

1 tablespoon margarine

1 (6-ounce) package seasoned stuffing mix

Bread slices, torn into small pieces (optional)

SUBMITTED BY:
Catherine Kercheval, Greensburg

America's
HOME COOKING

Chicken Enchilada Casserole

DIRECTIONS

Preheat oven to 375 degrees. Bake or skillet-fry chicken, reserving drippings. Chop chicken and mix with drippings, soup, chilies, onions and spices. Set aside. Soften tortillas in small amount of oil in a hot skillet; drain on paper towels. Place 3 tortillas in bottom of casserole dish, overlapping as needed. Pour 1/3 of soup and chicken mixture over tortillas. Add 1/3 of shredded cheese. Continue with 2 more layers, ending with soup and cheese on top. Bake for 35 to 40 minutes. Serves 8.

VARIATION

The corn tortillas can be chopped and about 12 ounces milk can be added to the soup mixture. Stir everything together in a large pot. Simmer on stove top and serve as chicken tortilla soup.

INGREDIENTS

4 chicken breasts

2 (10 1/2-ounce) cans cream of chicken soup

2 (4-ounce) cans chopped green chilies

2 large onions, coarsely diced

1/2 teaspoon oregano

1/2 teaspoon cumin

1/4 teaspoon sage

1/4 teaspoon chili powder

2 cloves garlic, pressed

1 (12-ounce) package corn tortillas

Cooking oil

1 to 1 1/2 pounds colby and monterey jack cheeses, shredded

Sour cream, for serving

SUBMITTED BY:
Julie Graham, Slippery Rock

Chicken Lo Mein

DIRECTIONS

About 45 minutes before serving, mix sliced chicken, soy sauce and cornstarch. Add a little water if too dry; set aside. Prepare linguini as directed; drain. Meanwhile, in a 12-inch skillet over medium heat in hot oil, cook mushrooms, onion, red pepper and Chinese pea pods. Stir quickly and frequently until tender crisp, about 3 to 5 minutes. Remove vegetables to a bowl with a slotted spoon. In the drippings left in the skillet, cook chicken mixture over high heat, stirring quickly and frequently, until chicken is tender (about 3 minutes). Return vegetables to the skillet; add chicken broth. Heat to boiling, stirring to loosen the brown bits at the skillet's bottom. Serves 6 with 330 calories per serving.

INGREDIENTS

2 large, skinless chicken breasts, cut into slivered pieces

3 tablespoons soy sauce

2 teaspoons cornstarch

1 (8-ounce) package linguini

1/4 cup oil

1/2 pound mushrooms, sliced

1 medium onion, chopped

1 large red pepper
(or 1/2 red pepper and 1/2 green pepper), thinly sliced

1 (6-ounce) bag frozen Chinese pea pods, thawed

1/2 cup chicken broth

SUBMITTED BY:
Rosemarie Weleski, Natrona Heights

America's
HOME COOKING

Chicken Loaf

DIRECTIONS

Preheat oven to 350 degrees. Mix eggs through chicken and place in a greased 8x8-inch pan. Mix topping ingredients and add to loaf. Cover and bake for 45 minutes. Uncover and bake additional 15 minutes. Let sit 15 minutes before serving.

INGREDIENTS

3 eggs, beaten

2 (10 1/2-ounce) cans chicken noodle soup, drained

1 (10 1/2-ounce) can cream of mushroom soup

1 (4-ounce) can mushrooms, drained

1 small onion, chopped

3 1/2 cup chopped almonds

4 cups dry stuffing mix

2 cups cut-up cooked chicken

TOPPING:

1 1/2 cups dry stuffing mix

4 tablespoons (1/2 stick) margarine, melted

Chicken broth

SUBMITTED BY:
Ruth Mason, Aliquippa

105

Chicken with Rice & Pignolia Nuts

DIRECTIONS

Sauté chicken and lamb in butter until browned. Remove from pan, add onion and sauté until soft. In another pan, toast the orzo in butter until nicely browned. Add the rice to the onions and sauté for a minute or two. Add the chicken and lamb back to the pan and season with the cumin, mint and pepper. Add the orzo and cover with chicken broth. Bring to a simmer, cover and simmer for approximately 20 minutes. Sprinkle with toasted pignolia nuts immediately before serving.

INGREDIENTS

4 boneless chicken breasts, thinly sliced

1 pound lamb, minced

2 tablespoons butter

1 large sweet onion, finely chopped

3 ounces orzo

2 cups basmati rice

2 teaspoons cumin, or more to taste

1 teaspoon dried mint

Fresh ground pepper, to taste

5 cups chicken broth

Toasted pignolia nuts

SUBMITTED BY:
Toni Orrico, Gibsonia

America's
HOME COOKING

Dad's Famous Slop

DIRECTIONS

Place all ingredients, except crackers, in a medium or large stockpot, depending on the amount of cabbage used. Add 1 cup water; cover. Place pot on stove over low heat for about 2 hours or until potatoes are soft, stirring occasionally. Cabbage will cook down and make liquid; do not add too much water. Serve with butter crackers. Serves 4.

INGREDIENTS

1 head cabbage, coarsely chopped

1 cup water

1 small onion, coarsely chopped

1 to 2 pounds kielbasa, sliced into 1-inch pieces

5 to 6 red skin potatoes, peeled and quartered

Butter crackers, for serving

SUBMITTED BY:
Mary Schmalzried, Finleyville

America's
HOME COOKING

Dad's Ham/Potato Casserole

DIRECTIONS

Preheat oven to 350 degrees. Prepare a 13x9-inch casserole with cooking spray. Mix ham, onions and potatoes in a large mixing bowl. Pour into prepared pan. Mix water and ketchup; pour over all. Cover with foil and bake for 30 minutes. Uncover and bake until potatoes are fork tender, about 30 to 45 additional minutes. Let sit for 5 minutes before serving.

INGREDIENTS

1 pound leftover ham, cubed

1 medium onion, diced

5 to 6 medium potatoes, peeled and sliced into 1/4-inch slices

1 cup water

1 cup ketchup

SUBMITTED BY:

Mary Irwin-Scott, Regent Square

Eye of Round Roast

DIRECTIONS

Preheat oven to 325 degrees. Brown roast in pan with shortening or olive oil. Remove roast and sauté mushrooms and onion in pan. Mix other ingredients in a roaster or Dutch oven. Add roast; pour liquid over roast. Cover with lid and place in oven. After 90 minutes, remove roast and turn on its other side. Baste roast and cook for 90 more minutes. At halfway point of cooking, add diced carrots and potatoes. Allow roast to sit for a few minutes before slicing. Spoon juices over roast.

NOTE

The sauce is wonderful on mashed potatoes. If there are any leftovers, save sauce with the meat.

INGREDIENTS

1 eye of round roast

Shortening or olive oil

1/2 pound mushrooms, sliced

1 large onion, chopped

1 tablespoon instant coffee granules

1 heaping teaspoon dijon or wine sauce mustard

2 (10 1/2-ounce) cans beef consommé

Carrots and potatoes, diced

SUBMITTED BY:
Mary Ellen Pampena, Allison Park

109

Grandma Tippy-Toe's Swiss Steak

DIRECTIONS

Trim steak of fat and cut into 6 to 8 equal pieces. Mix flour, salt and pepper. Place an 18-inch piece of foil on counter and sprinkle with 2 tablespoons of the seasoned flour. Dredge each piece of meat in flour and pound with the bumpy side of meat mallet until pieces are about 1/2 inch thick and coated in flour. Heat 1 tablespoon oil in Dutch oven or deep sauté pan over medium heat. Add meat, a few pieces at a time and brown well on both sides, adding more oil if necessary. Remove to a platter and continue frying until all meat has been browned and removed from pan. Add mushrooms to pan and sauté until they become soft, about 5 to 6 minutes. Remove mushrooms and add mushroom soup and milk. Stir until smooth. Add mushrooms, meat and any juices back into pot and stir well. Cover and cook, simmering lightly for 1 1/2 to 2 hours, or until meat is fall-apart tender. Serve over mashed potatoes.

INGREDIENTS

1 1/2 pounds round steak

1/2 cup flour

1 teaspoon salt

1/2 teaspoon pepper

1 to 2 tablespoons vegetable oil

8 ounces mushrooms, sliced

1 (10 1/2-ounce) can cream of mushroom soup

3/4 cup milk

Mashed potatoes, for serving

SUBMITTED BY:
Kimberlee Love, North Side

America's
HOME COOKING

Grandma's Meatloaf

DIRECTIONS

Preheat oven to 400 degrees. To make sauce, mix steak sauce with tomato sauce. Set aside. To form meatloaf, mix all remaining ingredients together with 1/2 sauce mixture. Blend well. Pat meatloaf into 9x5x3-inch greased loaf pan or shape into loaf and place in greased shallow baking pan. Spread remaining sauce over top of meatloaf. Bake for 1 hour.

NOTE

Meatloaf is sliced easily when cold. Chill, slice and microwave before serving. This meatloaf freezes very well.

INGREDIENTS

2 teaspoons steak sauce

1 (8-ounce) can tomato sauce

2 pounds ground beef, or 1 pound each ground beef and ground pork

2 teaspoons salt

1 cup breadcrumbs

2 eggs

3/4 cup milk

3 tablespoons parsley flakes

1 small onion, diced

1/4 cup shredded carrots

SUBMITTED BY:
Gloria Kelly, Ben Avon

Ham Balls

DIRECTIONS

Preheat oven to 350 degrees. Mix together the first 3 ingredients and form into balls. Put in a 9x13-inch glass baking dish. Mix together the last 3 ingredients in saucepan. Bring to a boil over medium-high heat while stirring or whisking. Pour over ham balls. Bake in oven until toothpick placed in ball comes out clean.

If ham loaf came with pineapple and cherries, chop these up and mix in with sauce.

INGREDIENTS

2 to 3 pounds ham loaf

2 large shredded wheat biscuits

1/2 cup milk

1 cup brown sugar

1/4 cup vinegar

2 teaspoons mustard

SUBMITTED BY:
Jennifer Potosky, Connellsville

Ham Hawaiian

DIRECTIONS

Melt the butter in a skillet and cook the ham, green pepper, onion and carrot for 5 minutes. Drain the pineapple, reserving the liquid from the pineapple. Mix the pineapple liquid with the brown sugar, cornstarch, vinegar, mustard, pepper and water. Stir this combination into skillet. Cook, stirring, until thickened. Add pineapple. Cook, stirring, for about 2 more minutes until hot all the way through. Serve with rice that has ground cloves added to it.

INGREDIENTS

2 tablespoons butter

2 cups slivered or diced cooked ham

1/2 medium green pepper, chopped

1 small or medium onion, sliced (optional)

1/2 carrot, cut into 1/4-inch rounds (optional)

1 (9-ounce) can pineapple chunks

2 tablespoons brown sugar

1 1/2 tablespoons cornstarch

1 1/2 tablespoons vinegar

1 1/2 teaspoons prepared mustard

Pepper, to taste

3/4 cup cold water

Ground cloves, to taste

Rice, for serving

SUBMITTED BY:
Scott Pavelle, Ross Township

113

Ham Loaf

DIRECTIONS

Mix meat with all ingredients, making 2 nice-sized loaves. Roll the loaves in extra graham cracker crumbs. Make sauce by bringing all sauce ingredients to a boil; keep warm while cooking loaves. Pour some sauce over loaves and bake in a slow oven for 2 hours. Serve sauce over ham slices as gravy.

INGREDIENTS

2 pounds ham, very finely ground

2 pounds pork, very finely ground

3 eggs

1 1/2 cups milk

3 cups graham crackers, finely crushed

SAUCE:

1 (10 3/4-ounce) can tomato soup

1/2 can water

1/2 cup vinegar

1 cup brown sugar

1 tablespoon dry mustard

SUBMITTED BY:
Eleanor Kells, Youngstown

America's
HOME COOKING

Hobo Stew

DIRECTIONS

Brown ground beef and bacon. Drain off fat. Add onion and green pepper and brown them. Add meat and put into a slow cooker. Drain each can of beans. Add to slow cooker. Stir in ketchup, brown sugar, salt and pepper, liquid smoke and vinegar. Stir, cover and cook for 4 to 9 hours.

INGREDIENTS

1 pound ground beef

1/2 pound bacon

1 cup chopped onion

1 cup chopped green pepper

2 (15-ounce) cans pork and beans

1 (15-ounce) can kidney beans

1 (15-ounce) can pinto beans

1 (15-ounce) can butter beans

1 cup ketchup

1/4 cup brown sugar

Salt and pepper, to taste

1 tablespoon liquid smoke (optional)

3 tablespoons apple cider vinegar

SUBMITTED BY:
Joyce Cress, Morgantown

Huffle Puffle

DIRECTIONS

Slice potatoes 1/8 inch thick. In a large cast iron skillet, fry potatoes until soft and brown. Season with salt and pepper, to taste. Add garlic, onion and green pepper. Add hot dogs. Once potatoes are done, fold mixture and let cook for 5 minutes. Crack eggs into a large bowl and pour in milk. Beat eggs and milk and pour over potatoes. Cover for 5 minutes, turning once. Cover for 3 minutes and then serve.

INGREDIENTS

5 large Idaho potatoes

Salt and pepper, to taste

Garlic powder, to taste

1 small onion, chopped (optional)

1/2 green pepper, chopped (optional)

10 all-beef hot dogs, sliced 1/8 inch thick

10 large eggs

1/4 cup milk

Ketchup or hot sauce, for serving

SUBMITTED BY:
William McCarty, Greensburg

America's
HOME COOKING

Italian Shepherd Pie

DIRECTIONS

Preheat oven to 375 degrees. In a skillet, cook sausage, onions and garlic until sausage is browned. Drain; stir in tomatoes, eggs, oregano, 3/4 cup of the cheddar cheese and 1/4 cup parmesan cheese. Pour into pie shell. Meanwhile, combine all the topping ingredients together. Pipe or spoon topping around edges of the pie. Bake for 50 to 55 minutes. Let stand 10 minutes before serving. Serves 8.

INGREDIENTS

1 pound Italian sausage

1/2 cup sliced green onions

2 cloves garlic, minced

1 (16-ounce) can Italian stewed tomatoes

3 eggs, beaten

3/4 teaspoon oregano, crushed

3/4 cup shredded cheddar cheese

1/4 cup parmesan cheese

1 (9-inch) unbaked pie shell

TOPPING:

2 cups mashed potatoes

1/2 cup shredded cheddar cheese

2 tablespoons parmesan cheese

1/2 teaspoon black pepper

SUBMITTED BY:
Kevin Sunderlin, DuBois

America's
HOME COOKING

Johnny Mayette, Revisited

DIRECTIONS

Preheat oven to 350 degrees. Brown pork until almost done; pour off most of the fat, leaving just enough to brown onion and green pepper, and complete the browning of the pork. Pour off any remaining fat. Cut up cream cheese and add to mixture in frying pan. Stir until all of the cream cheese has melted into the mixture. In a large greased casserole dish, alternately add meat mixture, noodles and undiluted soup and/or tomatoes. Mix together thoroughly. Cover and bake for 45 to 60 minutes, or until casserole is bubbly and crispy around the edges.

INGREDIENTS

1 1/2 to 2 pounds ground pork

1 medium onion, diced

1 green pepper, diced

1 (8-ounce) package cream cheese, softened to room temperature

2 cups egg noodles, cooked and drained

1 to 2 (10 3/4-ounce) cans tomato soup, or 1 can soup and 1 (10 1/2-ounce) can diced tomatoes with basil, garlic and oregano

SUBMITTED BY:
Nancy Shaffner, Pittsburgh

Karin's Chicken Divan

DIRECTIONS

Preheat oven to 375 degrees. Cook rice according to package directions; set aside. Cut chicken into 3/4-inch strips. Grease skillet and lightly cook chicken strips. Salt and pepper chicken to taste. Grease square 2-quart casserole dish with cooking spray. Press rice evenly into bottom of dish. Lay chicken pieces evenly to cover rice. In a small bowl, combine mayonnaise and broccoli soup. Stir in curry powder and lemon juice. Mix well, set aside. Cover chicken completely with frozen broccoli florets. Spoon sauce over frozen broccoli and spread around to completely cover casserole. Cover top with shredded cheddar cheese. Bake for 30 minutes.

INGREDIENTS

2 cups uncooked white rice

2 to 3 boneless, skinless chicken breasts

Salt and pepper, to taste

1/2 cup mayonnaise

1 (10 1/2-ounce) can cream of broccoli soup

1/2 teaspoon curry powder

1 tablespoon lemon juice

1 (16-ounce) bag frozen broccoli florets

1 1/2 cups shredded cheddar cheese

Nonstick cooking spray

SUBMITTED BY:
Carrie Zahniser, Forest Hills

119

Kennywood Picnic City Chicken Sticks

DIRECTIONS

If necessary, cut cubes to uniform size. (If preferred, for pork, buy boneless western-style ribs and cut into cubes of desired size.) Alternate meat cubes on skewers, beginning and ending with pork, placing a square of onion between cubes. Sprinkle seasonings on all sides. Dust all sides with flour.

In a rectangular dish, whisk eggs with 2 tablespoons oil. In another dish, add bread-crumbs. Dip each stick in egg, allowing excess to drip off. Roll and shake in the breadcrumbs. Place on tray. Set tray of breaded sticks in refrigerator for about 30 minutes.

Preheat roaster to 350 degrees. In large skillet in hot oil, gently brown sticks on all sides; do not crowd. Place browned sticks in roaster on crumpled foil. Bake covered for about 1 1/4 to 1 1/2 hours.

INGREDIENTS

12 6-inch wooden skewers

2 pounds pork cubes

1 pound veal cubes

1 large sweet onion, separate each layer and cut into 1-inch squares

Onion powder, to taste

Garlic powder, to taste

Salt and pepper, to taste

Paprika, to taste

Flour, for dusting

3 eggs

Vegetable or canola oil

Italian-seasoned breadcrumbs

SUBMITTED BY:
Chris Bobick, Chalk Hill

America's
HOME COOKING

Mazetti

DIRECTIONS

Brown meat and add garlic, vegetables and water. Cover and steam until vegetables are tender. Remove from heat. Cook noodles until al dente; drain. Add to meat mixture; mix in soup, undrained mushrooms, parsley, salt and pepper. Coat a 3-quart casserole dish with non-stick cooking spray and pour mixture into it. Sprinkle with cheese. Place in a cold oven, turn oven to 250 degrees. Bake uncovered for 1 hour or until bubbly. Serves 10 to 12.

INGREDIENTS

2 pounds ground beef

2 cloves garlic, minced

1 1/2 cup chopped onions

2 1/2 cups finely chopped celery

1/2 cup chopped green pepper

2 tablespoons water

1 (8-ounce) package medium noodles

2 (10 3/4-ounce) cans condensed tomato soup

1 (6-ounce) can mushrooms with liquid

1 teaspoon parsley

2 teaspoons salt

1 teaspoon pepper

2 cups shredded cheddar cheese

SUBMITTED BY:
Kevin Sunderlin, DuBois

America's
HOME COOKING

Meatloaf Japanese Style

DIRECTIONS

Preheat oven to 375 degrees. Mix all ingredients except sesame. Place in a pan and put in oven. Cook for 20 minutes. Sprinkle sesame on top. Cook another 5 minutes.

INGREDIENTS

1 pound minced chicken meat

1/2 onion, chopped

1/2 carrot, chopped

3 shiitake mushrooms, chopped

20 green peas

1 egg

1/2 cup breadcrumbs

2 tablespoons miso

1/2 tablespoon sake

1/2 tablespoon soy sauce

1 tablespoon light soy sauce

1/2 teaspoon salt

Pepper, to taste

Ginger water

1/2 tablespoon black sesame

1/2 tablespoon white sesame

SUBMITTED BY:
Mihoko Pooley, Oakland

Missouri

DIRECTIONS

Preheat oven to 375 degrees. In the bottom of a 13x9-inch glass baking dish, pat a thin layer of the ground meat. Put a thin layer of 1/3 of the sliced potatoes and 1/3 of the sliced onions on top of the meat. Add salt and pepper. Repeat for two more layers, ending with potato and onion layer. Pour crushed tomatoes over the meat, potatoes and onion. Sprinkle the top generously with celery seed. Cover casserole with foil and bake for 1 1/2 to 2 hours or until potatoes are fork tender.

INGREDIENTS

1 1/2 pounds ground meat

4 to 5 large potatoes, peeled and thinly sliced

1 medium onion, thinly sliced

Salt and pepper, to taste

1 (28-ounce) can crushed tomatoes

1 tablespoon celery seed

SUBMITTED BY:
Hilary Zubritzky, McKees Rocks

Mustard Chicken or One-Pot Chicken

DIRECTIONS

Rinse chicken breasts and make sure they are not too thick. If thick, slice them down in size. Lay the chicken breasts flat and place 1/4 to 1/2 teaspoon of mustard on each breast. Roll the breast up and use 1 or 2 toothpicks to secure the breast. Melt margarine in large nonstick pot. Place chicken breasts in pot and brown them slightly. Remove from pot. Place flavored rice mix in pot and brown. Place three cups of warm water in pot with rice and add flavor packet, carrots and chicken. Cook, covered, for 1 hour or until all the water is absorbed and the rice and chicken are done. Stir the rice and turn the chicken occasionally to prevent burning.

INGREDIENTS

4 to 6 boneless chicken breasts

Spicy mustard

3 teaspoons margarine

1 (6.9-ounce) box chicken-flavored rice and vermicelli mix

3 cups water

1 cup carrots

SUBMITTED BY:
Terri Laver

124

Oven-Fried Chicken

DIRECTIONS

Preheat oven to 350 or 375 degrees. Place chicken in shallow dish. Cover with skim milk. Soak 15 to 20 minutes. Combine remaining ingredients to make a crumb mixture. Shake off milk from each piece and dip in crumbs. Coat a shallow pan with nonstick cooking spray and place chicken in it. (Pan can be lined with foil for easy clean up.) Spray chicken pieces lightly with cooking spray. Bake for 40 to 50 minutes.

INGREDIENTS

12 chicken legs and thighs, skinned

Skim milk

1/2 cup grated parmesan cheese

2 cups crushed corn flakes

1 tablespoon dried parsley

Paprika, to taste

Thyme, to taste

SUBMITTED BY:
Catherine Kercheval, Greensburg

America's
HOME COOKING

Pan De Elote

DIRECTIONS

Preheat oven to 400 degrees. Combine batter ingredients (corn through milk). Pour half into a well-greased 8x8-inch glass baking dish. Cover with chilies and cheese. Spread remaining batter on top. Bake, uncovered, for 35 to 45 minutes until brown on top.

NOTE

For an extra kick, use pepper jack cheese instead of monterey jack cheese.

INGREDIENTS

1 (1-pound) can cream-style corn

1 cup baking mix

1 egg, beaten

2 tablespoons melted butter

2 tablespoons sugar

1/2 cup milk

1 (4-ounce) can chopped green chilies

1/2 pound monterey jack cheese, thinly sliced

SUBMITTED BY:
Amy Molinaro, Pittsburgh

America's HOME COOKING

Paprika Schnitzel

DIRECTIONS

Dice bacon and fry until crisp. Remove bacon from pan and add diced onion and cook until translucent. Salt and pepper the meat and dredge in flour. Place in skillet with onion and fry on both sides until brown. Remove meat from pan and set aside. In a bowl, mix sour cream, tomato soup or sauce and paprika, and mix well. Add bacon back to the onion in the skillet (add garlic or more paprika, if desired) and add the sauce. Heat until warm and add browned meat. Simmer for 20 to 40 minutes. Serve schnitzel with mashed potatoes, buttered noodles or rice.

INGREDIENTS

1/2 pound bacon

1 large onion, diced

Salt and pepper, to taste

Flour, to dust meat

1 pound veal or thinly cut pork chops

1 (8-ounce) container sour cream

1 (10 3/4-ounce) can tomato soup or sauce

2 tablespoons paprika

Garlic (optional)

Mashed potatoes, buttered noodles or rice, for serving

SUBMITTED BY:
Monica Narr, Crafton

America's
HOME COOKING

Pastor Matt's Shepherd Pie

DIRECTIONS

Brown meat, drain and place in bottom a 9x13-inch baking pan. Preheat oven to 350 degrees. In a small skillet, sauté mushrooms and onions in butter. When onions are translucent, layer on top of meat. Mix soup according to can directions and add to pan. Spread mashed potatoes over soup and top with cheddar cheese. Bake until cheese is melted. Serve with a loaf of homemade bread.

INGREDIENTS

1 1/2 to 2 pounds ground beef or sausage

1 tablespoon butter

8 mushrooms, sliced

1 medium onion, chopped

1 (10 1/2-ounce) can cheddar cheese soup

8 large potatoes, cooked and mashed

1 pound cheddar cheese, shredded

1 loaf homemade bread, for serving

SUBMITTED BY:
Matthew Potosky, Connellsville

America's HOME COOKING

Polpette

DIRECTIONS

Peel and quarter potatoes. Boil in salted water about 20 minutes, or until tender. Drain and press through a ricer or mash well. Set aside and allow to cool. Mix ground meat with seasoned breadcrumbs, cheese, eggs, onion and seasonings. Add cooled potatoes (or cold leftover mashed potatoes) and mix. Form into oval-shaped meatballs, about 2 to 3 inches long, and roll in plain breadcrumbs. Fry in hot olive oil, turning frequently, until browned on all sides and cooked through to center. Makes about 12 meatballs.

INGREDIENTS

2 medium potatoes

1 pound very lean ground beef

1/2 cup seasoned breadcrumbs

3 to 4 tablespoons grated parmesan cheese

2 eggs, slightly beaten

1/2 cup finely chopped onion

1 tablespoon chopped fresh parsley

1 teaspoon garlic powder

Salt and pepper, to taste

Dash of nutmeg, to taste

1 cup plain breadcrumbs

1/2 cup olive oil (approximate)

SUBMITTED BY:
Marlene McGaffic, McMurray

America's
HOME COOKING

Pork Chops with Ketchup

DIRECTIONS

Rinse chops and pat dry. Season well with salt and pepper. Heat oil in a nonstick skillet over medium-high heat. Brown chops, 3 at a time. While chops brown, mix 2 cups ketchup with 1/2 cup water in a large slow cooker. Add chops and stir. Pour off any fat from skillet and add remaining 1 cup ketchup and 1/3 cup water. Stir to deglaze pan. Pour over chops in slow cooker. Cook on low for 5 to 7 hours and serve over steamed rice.

INGREDIENTS

6 bone-in pork chops

Salt and pepper, to taste

2 tablespoons oil

3 cups ketchup

Water

Rice, steamed, for serving

SUBMITTED BY:
Kimberlee Love, North Side

Pork Snitzel

DIRECTIONS

Place cutlets between wax paper and pound thin. Cut small slits around edges of chops to prevent curling. Mix flour, seasoned salt and pepper in 1 bowl. Mix eggs and milk in another. Mix breadcrumbs and paprika in a third bowl. Dip cutlets in flour, then egg mix and finally breadcrumbs. Melt shortening in skillet and cook cutlets until no longer pink, about 10 to 15 minutes. Remove from skillet and set aside. Combine 2 tablespoons flour and dill weed; add to skillet. Add broth to skillet. Stir well, loosening all brown bits from the pan. Add sour cream and heat through. Serve sauce on the side with meat.

NOTE

The sauce also is good with noodles or potatoes as a side dish.

INGREDIENTS

6 boneless pork loin cutlets

1/2 cup flour

2 teaspoons seasoned salt

1/2 teaspoon pepper

2 eggs

1/4 cup milk

1/2 cup fine breadcrumbs

2 teaspoons paprika

6 tablespoons shortening

2 tablespoons flour

1/2 to 1 teaspoon dill weed

1 1/2 cups chicken broth

1 cup sour cream, at room temperature

SUBMITTED BY:
Joann Sklarsky, Johnstown

America's
HOME COOKING

Pork-Q-Pine Balls

DIRECTIONS

Preheat oven to 400 degrees. Mix ground pork, rice, egg, breadcrumbs, seasonings and 2 tablespoons of the crushed pineapple. Form into balls. Place on cookie sheet and bake for 10 minutes or until brown; remove to paper towels to absorb excess fat. Decrease oven temperature to 300 degrees. In an ovenproof pan, spread a thin layer of barbecue sauce, place pork balls on top, pour the rest of the crushed pineapple on top of pork balls and finally pour the remainder of the barbecue sauce on top of the pineapples. Cover and bake for 1 hour. Serve as appetizers on a buffet table or over white or brown rice as a main dish.

INGREDIENTS

2 pounds ground pork

2 cups cooked rice

1 egg, beaten

1 cup unseasoned breadcrumbs

1 tablespoon salt

1 tablespoon black pepper

1 teaspoon onion powder

1 teaspoon garlic powder

1/4 teaspoon ground cloves

1 (20-ounce) can crushed pineapple

1 (18-ounce) bottle barbecue sauce

White or brown rice, for serving

SUBMITTED BY:
Monica Narr, Crafton

America's
HOME COOKING

Real Gone Barbecued Pot Roast

DIRECTIONS

Brown meat in oil. Discard the oil and put meat in a deep roasting pan. Sprinkle liberally with salt and pepper. Add the tomato sauce, garlic and onion slices into the pan. Fill the tomato sauce can with water and add water to the pan. Cover and simmer for 1 1/2 to 2 hours. Add remaining ingredients. Cook for another 1 1/2 hours, stirring occasionally and adding water if necessary. Skim fat and serve with rice or noodles.

INGREDIENTS

1/4 cup oil

4 pounds beef roast

Salt and pepper, to taste

1 (8-ounce) can tomato sauce

2 cloves garlic, minced

3 to 4 onions, depending on size, sliced

2 tablespoons brown sugar

1/2 teaspoon dry mustard

1/4 cup lemon juice

1/4 cup white vinegar

1/4 cup ketchup

1 tablespoon worcestershire sauce

2 teaspoons hot sauce

Rice or noodles, for serving

SUBMITTED BY:
Scott Pavelle, Ross Township

America's
HOME COOKING

Saturday Buried Treasure

DIRECTIONS

Preheat oven to 350 degrees. Grease a 9x13-inch casserole dish and set aside. Boil water with salt; add pasta and cook. Drain and set aside. Heat milk in a saucepan and, when boiling, add cornstarch to create a roux. When sauce is thickened, add diced up pasteurized process cheese and mix. Season with salt, black pepper and cayenne pepper, to taste. Add pasta to cheese sauce and mix thoroughly. Spread 1/3 of the pasta mixture in bottom of 9x13-inch pan. Next, layer the diced leftover meat which can be one item or a combination of meats. Top meat layer with another layer of cheesy pasta and then layer leftover vegetables on top of pasta. Top vegetables with the last 1/3 of cheesy pasta and finish with grated cheese. Bake, covered, for 30 to 40 minutes. Serve with salad or garlic bread.

NOTE

This recipe uses items that have been "buried" in the refrigerator during the week and has a lot of flexibility. Examples of "buried treasure" include diced chicken combined with leftover salsa or pizza sauce or ground meat and/or sausage combined with spaghetti sauce or sloppy joe mix.

SUBMITTED BY:
Monica Narr, Crafton

INGREDIENTS

1 pound pasta

3 cups milk

1/4 cup cornstarch

1 (8-ounce) block of pasteurized process cheese, diced

Salt and black pepper, to taste

Cayenne pepper, to taste

2 cups diced leftover meat of choice

2 cups leftover vegetables of choice

Grated cheese of choice

Leftover jars of salsa or sauces

Sauerkraut Casserole

DIRECTIONS

Preheat oven to 350 degrees. Brown loose sausage while cooking egg noodles. Drain noodles and sausage. Mix together; add sauerkraut and brown sugar. Bake, covered, for 20 to 30 minutes.

INGREDIENTS

1 (16-ounce) package loose sausage

1 (12-ounce) bag egg noodles

1 pound package sauerkraut, drained

1/2 to 1 cup brown sugar

SUBMITTED BY:
Jennifer Potosky, Connellsville

Sicilian Steak

DIRECTIONS

Preheat the oven to 350 degrees. Cut steaks into 4-ounce portions and pound thin. Combine breadcrumbs with oregano and cheese. Dip meat in egg wash and then in crumbs. Grease a pan with olive oil and place meat in it. Mix the relish ingredients together and top each steak with the mixture. Cook for 20 minutes and then broil for 10 minutes to roast the vegetables.

INGREDIENTS

1 pound round steak, pounded thin

1/2 cup Italian-seasoned breadcrumbs

1/2 teaspoon oregano

1/4 cup parmesan cheese

1 egg, beaten with water

RELISH:

1/4 cup chopped fresh parsley

1/4 cup chopped sweet onion

1/4 cup chopped tomatoes

1/4 cup chopped green pepper

1 clove garlic, finely minced

Pinch of salt

Red pepper flakes

3 tablespoons olive oil

SUBMITTED BY:
Nina Mule Lyons, Pittsburgh

136

Slow Cooked Glazed Ham

DIRECTIONS

Pour ginger ale or lemon-lime soda pop into a large slow cooker. Place ham in slow cooker. Cook on high for 2 hours. Reduce setting to low and cook an additional 4 hours. At end of the low-heat cooking time, preheat oven to 450 degrees. Spray a baking dish or roaster with nonstick spray. Carefully remove ham from slow cooker and place in a baking dish. Combine brown sugar with enough orange juice to make a paste. Spread paste over ham to completely cover. Bake 15 to 20 minutes or until lightly browned. Remove ham carefully onto carving surface. Slice or pull apart according to preference. Arrange serving platter with garnishes of fresh parsley, cherries and orange slices.

NOTE

A gravy may be made from the ham juices. Also, a raisin sauce may be served on the side during formal occasions for added decadence.

INGREDIENTS

1 (2-liter) bottle ginger ale or lemon-lime soda pop

1 good-quality whole or half ham

1 to 2 cups brown sugar

Orange juice, just enough to form a paste

1 bunch curly parsley, for garnishing

1 pint fresh cherries, for garnishing

1 orange, sliced, for garnishing

SUBMITTED BY:
Lisa Lopez Ramirez, Kittanning

Spiedini

DIRECTIONS

Freeze the eye of round overnight and then allow to thaw in the refrigerator the next day. (This will make it possible to cut the thinnest slices of beef.) Slice meat as thinly as possible; if a slicing machine is available, set it at 1/16 of an inch. Mix 1 1/2 cups of the breadcrumbs with all the remaining dry ingredients. Moisten with lemon juice and enough oil to make a paste. Lay out slices of the beef and top with a teaspoon of the breadcrumb mixture, a sliver of mozzarella and a sliver of tomato. Roll up into an oblong bundle, tucking in the sides. Put roll onto a skewer, securing the end. Put 4 or 5 spiedini on each skewer. Dip the completed skewers in olive oil and coat with the remaining breadcrumbs. Barbecue or broil in the oven for 3 to 4 minutes per side.

INGREDIENTS

4 to 5 pounds beef eye of round

3 cups breadcrumbs

Pinch of oregano

Pinch of basil

Salt and pepper

1 tablespoon parsley

Juice of 1 lemon

Olive oil

1/2 pound mozzarella, cut into slivers

2 small tomatoes, cut into slivers

SUBMITTED BY:
Chris Fennimore, "QED Cooks"

Steak, Bacon & Macaroni

DIRECTIONS

Fry bacon until crisp. Add steak and brown
well. Add tomato soup; mix well. Add 1/4 can
of water. Lower heat and cover. Simmer until
steak is tender (about 15 minutes). Add cooked
macaroni and stir until blended.

INGREDIENTS

8 to 10 slices bacon,
cut into 1-inch pieces

1 pound sirloin tip steak,
cut into 1-inch cubes

1 (10 3/4-ounce) can tomato
soup

1/4 can water

2 cups cooked elbow
macaroni

SUBMITTED BY:
Deborah Stacy, Oakdale

139

Stuffed Bread

DIRECTIONS

Preheat oven to 350 degrees. In a skillet, soften the onion and garlic, add the chicken and cook chicken pieces until no longer pink. Add bag of broccoli, cover skillet and let cook until broccoli is no longer frozen. Drain and let filling cool slightly. While filling is cooling, spray a baking sheet with nonstick cooking spray and open 2 cans of rolls. Lay out the dough to form 1 layer. Sprinkle ranch dressing evenly over the dough. Cut cream cheese into small pieces and arrange on the dough. When filling is cool enough to handle, spread filling evenly on the prepared dough. Sprinkle with cheddar cheese. Top with the remaining cans of rolls and seal edges by pressing dough together. Bake for 30 minutes or until the rolls are done. Cut into wedges and serve.

INGREDIENTS

1 medium onion, chopped

2 tablespoons chopped garlic, or to taste

4 chicken breasts, or equivalent of other boneless chicken, cut

1 (16-ounce) bag frozen chopped broccoli

4 (8-ounce) cans crescent rolls

Ranch dressing mix

1 (8-ounce) or 2 (3-ounce) packages cream cheese

2 to 3 cups shredded cheddar cheese

VARIATION

This recipe can be increased or decreased by varying the number of packages of rolls used and the amount of filling made. Other filling combinations also work well. Cheese may be all of one type or a mixture of cheeses.

SUBMITTED BY:
Sharon Morford, North Hills

Stuffed Cabbage

DIRECTIONS

Preheat oven to 350 degrees. Mix ground beef or veal, pork, rice, eggs, onions, garlic, salt and pepper. Cut around the core of the cabbage with a knife, but do not remove the core. Place the entire head of cabbage in a large pot of hot, but not boiling, water. Gently peel off the cabbage leaves as the cabbage cooks and softens. Place about 1/4 cup of the meat mixture in a cabbage leaf and roll up. (As the cabbage leaves get smaller, they will become harder to roll.) Shred any remaining cabbage left on the heads. In a roasting pan, place 3 strips bacon on the bottom. Place 1/2 of the leftover shredded cabbage on top of the bacon. Place the stuffed cabbages on top of the shredded cabbage and then place the remaining shredded cabbage on top of the stuffed cabbages. Add 1 can of water to the tomato soup and pour soup and crushed tomatoes over stuffed cabbages. Bake for approximately 2 hours. Makes about 2 dozen cabbage rolls.

INGREDIENTS

2 pounds ground veal or beef

1 pound ground pork

1 cup cooked white rice

2 eggs

2 small onions, finely chopped

1 clove garlic, finely chopped

1 teaspoon salt

1/2 teaspoon pepper

2 medium-size heads cabbage

1 (10 3/4-ounce) can tomato soup

1 (14-ounce) can crushed tomatoes

3 strips bacon

SUBMITTED BY:
Marian Taylor, Penn Hills

America's
HOME COOKING

141

Stuffed Peppers (European Style)

DIRECTIONS

Preheat oven to 350 degrees. Sauté onions and garlic in margarine. Set aside. Finely dice kielbasa and set aside. Cut tops from peppers, removing seeds and ribs. Combine ground beef, salt, pepper, egg, rice and onion and garlic mixture and half of the chopped kielbasa. Mix well. Fill peppers. Drain sauerkraut. Mix with stewed tomatoes. Layer half of sauerkraut mixture in bottom of baking dish. Place stuffed peppers on sauerkraut. Sprinkle the remaining kielbasa between peppers. Cover with remaining sauerkraut mixture. Bake for 2 hours.

INGREDIENTS

2 small onions, chopped

2 cloves garlic, chopped

2 tablespoons margarine

1/2 pound kielbasa

6 medium green peppers

1 1/2 pounds ground beef

3/4 teaspoon salt

1/2 teaspoon pepper

1 egg

1/2 cup uncooked rice

1 (16-ouncc) can sauerkraut

2 cups stewed tomatoes

SUBMITTED BY:
Marge Samek, Monroeville

Sweet and Sour Meatballs with Cabbage

DIRECTIONS

Combine ground beef, salt, pepper, eggs, onion and oats. Shape into small balls. In a large soup pot or Dutch oven, combine chili sauce, grape jelly, brown sugar and apricot nectar. Bring to a boil; add meatballs and place cabbage on top. Lower heat and simmer, covered, stirring occasionally, for 2 hours. Serves 6 to 8.

INGREDIENTS

2 pounds ground beef

1 teaspoon salt

1/2 teaspoon pepper

2 eggs, beaten

1 tablespoon instant minced onion, or 1/4 cup fresh minced onion

1/4 cup quick oats

1 (12-ounce) bottle chili sauce

1 (12-ounce) jar grape jelly

3 tablespoons brown sugar

1/4 cup apricot nectar or orange juice

1 small head cabbage, coarsely chopped

SUBMITTED BY:
Susan Cohen, Pittsburgh

Swiss Smoked Turkey Bake

DIRECTIONS

Preheat oven to 400 degrees. Cook onion in 2 tablespoons butter until tender. Do not burn. Stir in flour, salt and pepper. Add undrained mushrooms, half & half or light cream, and wine. Stir until thickened. Add turkey and ham, or just turkey, and water chestnuts. Pour into 2-quart oval or rectangular ovenproof casserole and sprinkle cheese on top. Combine soft breadcrumbs and melted butter. Sprinkle on top of casserole. Bake for 20 to 25 minutes, until lightly brown. Serves 6.

NOTE

If ham is not desired in the recipe, simply use 3 instead of 2 cups of smoked turkey.

INGREDIENTS

1/2 cup onion, diced

2 tablespoons butter

3 tablespoons flour

1/2 teaspoon salt

1/2 teaspoon pepper

1(3-ounce) can sliced mushrooms, undrained

1 cup half & half or light cream

2 tablespoons white wine

2 cups smoked turkey, cut in chunks

1 cup ham, cut in chunks

1 (5-ounce) can sliced water chestnuts, drained

1 cup shredded Swiss cheese

2 cups soft breadcrumbs

4 tablespoons butter, melted

SUBMITTED BY:
Roberta Bauer, Wexford

America's
HOME COOKING

Szekely Gulyas

DIRECTIONS

In skillet, sauté onions in margarine. Add pork and brown. Add veal and brown. Add kraut; cover and simmer 30 minutes or until meat is tender. Blend together tomato puree, sour cream, broth and flour. Pour over skillet mixture. Simmer, stirring frequently, for 10 minutes. Serves 4 to 6.

NOTE

This recipe can also be made in a slow cooker. Place sautéed onions and browned meat in slow cooker. Add remaining ingredients and cook on low for 6 hours or until meat is tender and mixture has thickened up a bit.

INGREDIENTS

1 1/4 cup chopped onions

2 tablespoons margarine

1 pound pork, cubed

1 pound veal, cubed

1 (16-ounce) can sauerkraut, drained

1/2 cup tomato puree

1 cup sour cream

1 cup beef broth

2 tablespoons flour

SUBMITTED BY:
Joann Sklarsky, Johnstown

Tangy Pork Chops

DIRECTIONS

Brown pork chops on both sides. On each chop, place an onion slice. On top of onion slice, place a lemon slice and 1 tablespoon brown sugar. Mix ketchup and water, pour over chops and reduce heat to simmer. Cover and cook for 1 hour. Remove lemon slices before serving.

NOTE

Sauce will be thin. For a thicker gravy, add a flour/water mixture and stir until desired thickness is reached.

INGREDIENTS

6 1/2 inch center-cut pork chops

1 onion, cut in 6 slices

1 lemon, cut in 6 slices

6 tablespoons brown sugar

1 cup ketchup

1 cup water

SUBMITTED BY:
Sally Milton, McKees Rocks

146

Turkey Tetrazinni

DIRECTIONS

Preheat oven to 400 degrees. To make cheese sauce, combine all sauce ingredients (milk through flour) in a saucepan. Cook on low until cheese is melted and ingredients are mixed well. Add cooked spaghetti to large mixing bowl. Mix soup, milk and cheese sauce together and add to spaghetti. Add turkey and mushrooms. Mix well so soup and cheese sauce cover all spaghetti noodles and meat and mushrooms are distributed throughout. Add more turkey and mushrooms if desired. Spray or rub a large, deep casserole bowl with cooking spray or butter. Add all ingredients to casserole dish. Sprinkle parmesan cheese on top. Bake for 30 to 35 minutes or until tetrazinni bubbles around the edges.

INGREDIENTS

1 pound thin spaghetti, cooked

1 (10 1/2-ounce) can cream of mushroom soup

1 1/2 cups milk

3 to 4 cups diced, leftover cooked turkey

4 ounces sliced fresh or canned mushrooms

3 tablespoons grated parmesan cheese

Cheese sauce (see below)

CHEESE SAUCE:

1 1/2 cups milk

1 cup cubed pasteurized process cheese

3 tablespoons butter

3 tablespoons flour

SUBMITTED BY:
Joann Sklarsky, Johnstown

Unstuffed Cabbage Casserole

DIRECTIONS

Preheat oven to 350 degrees. Brown ground meat with onion powder or chopped onion. Stir uncooked rice into meat. Divide chopped cabbage into thirds. Layer as follows in a 13x9-inch pan: 1/3 cabbage, 1/3 sauerkraut and 1/2 meat mixture. Repeat layers until ingredients are all used, ending with cabbage and sauerkraut. Mix soup, water, salt and pepper. Pour over casserole. Cover with foil and bake for 1 1/2 hours. Remove foil during last 1/2 hour of cooking time.

INGREDIENTS

1 1/2 pounds ground beef

Onion powder or chopped onion

1/2 cup uncooked rice

1 head cabbage, chopped

1 (14-ounce) can sauerkraut

2 (10 3/4-ounce) cans tomato soup

1 1/2 cups water

Salt and pepper, to taste

SUBMITTED BY:
Mary Dawson, Poland

Upside Down Pizza Pie

DIRECTIONS

Preheat oven to 350 degrees. Brown beef in large skillet. Remove from heat and drain fat. Let stand 3 to 5 minutes to cool slightly. Add all but 1 tablespoon of eggs to beef. Stir in pizza or spaghetti sauce until well blended. Spread mixture in an ungreased 9x13x2-inch baking dish. Sprinkle with cheddar cheese and arrange mozzarella on top. For crust, unroll dough on a lightly floured surface. Firmly press edges and perforations to seal. Roll to form a 13x9-inch rectangle. Place over cheese and brush with reserved beaten egg. Bake for 20 minutes. Let stand 5 minutes before cutting into squares. Serves 8 to 12.

INGREDIENTS

2 pounds lean ground beef

2 large eggs, slightly beaten

1 (15-1/2 ounce) jar pizza or spaghetti sauce

2 cups shredded cheddar cheese

8 ounces sliced mozzarella cheese

1 (8-ounce) can refrigerated crescent dinner rolls

SUBMITTED BY:
Peg Bittner, South Park

America's
HOME COOKING

Vegetables

Baked Mushroom Casserole

DIRECTIONS

Preheat oven to 350 degrees. Sauté onion and fresh mushrooms in butter or margarine for 4 to 5 minutes. Combine the remaining ingredients in a bowl. Add to the onion and mushroom mixture. Mix well and pour into a greased 1 1/2-quart casserole dish. Bake for 30 minutes, covered. Remove cover and bake for an additional 30 minutes. Let set 5 minutes before serving.

NOTE

This casserole is great when served with any type of meat, chicken or fish. Also, it is a good side dish and great as leftovers.

INGREDIENTS

1 large onion, chopped

1 pound fresh mushrooms, sliced, or 4 (4-ounce) cans, drained

1/4 cup butter or margarine

1 cup cracker crumbs

2 eggs, beaten

1/2 cup cream

1/2 teaspoon salt

4 ounces cheddar cheese, shredded

SUBMITTED BY:
Frank Hilliard, East Liverpool

152

Broccoli Casserole

DIRECTIONS

Preheat oven to 350 degrees. Combine broccoli through cheese; mix well. Pour mixture into 1 1/2-quart casserole dish. Mix crushed butter crackers and melted butter; sprinkle mix on top of casserole. Bake for 45 minutes.

INGREDIENTS

1 (10-ounce) package broccoli, cooked

1 (10 1/2-ounce) can mushroom soup, undiluted

2 tablespoons dried onions

3 tablespoons mayonnaise

1 egg, beaten

1/2 cup shredded sharp cheese

Butter crackers, crushed

Melted butter

SUBMITTED BY:
Mrs. R. W. Brownlee, Washington

153

Eggplant Casserole

DIRECTIONS

Preheat oven to 350 degrees. Slice eggplant with skin on, then cut into 1-inch cubes. Cook in boiling water until eggplant is fairly soft, about 15 minutes. In a skillet, cook bacon until brown and break into 1-inch pieces (or slice the bacon into 1-inch strips before cooking). Drain off most of bacon grease, but leave enough to sauté onions. Put eggplant, onions and bacon into an ungreased casserole dish. Add chopped tomatoes and reserved tomato juice to casserole. Break up bread into small pieces and mix into casserole. Add enough shredded cheese to cover top of casserole. Bake until casserole is cooked through and cheese is bubbly, about 30 minutes.

NOTE

This casserole can be used as a main dish with a salad and baked potatoes or rice on the side, or as a side dish with a chicken, fish or pork entree.

INGREDIENTS

1 large eggplant

8 or 16 ounces bacon

1 medium or large yellow onion, sliced and cut into small pieces

1 (5-ounce) can whole tomatoes, chopped, reserve juice

2 to 3 slices whole wheat bread

Medium or sharp cheddar cheese, shredded

SUBMITTED BY:
Diane Mercer, Pittsburgh

America's
HOME COOKING

English Walnut Broccoli

DIRECTIONS

Preheat oven to 350 degrees. Cook broccoli in salted water until tender, drain and put into a greased 1 1/2-quart oblong casserole. In a saucepan, melt 1/2 cup butter, whisk in flour and chicken base or bouillon cubes, and stir to make a smooth paste. Gradually add milk, cook and stir until thick and smooth. Pour sauce evenly over broccoli. Heat 2/3 cup water and 6 tablespoons butter until butter melts. Pour over stuffing mix and toss to coat. Add walnuts to stuffing and toss again. Top broccoli mixture with stuffing mix. Bake 30 minutes. Serves 8.

INGREDIENTS

2 (10-ounce) packages frozen chopped broccoli

1/2 cup butter

4 tablespoons flour

1 1/2 tablespoons chicken base or 4 crushed chicken bouillon cubes

2 cups milk

2/3 cup water

6 tablespoons butter

2/3 (8-ounce) package herb stuffing mix

2/3 cup coarsely chopped walnuts

SUBMITTED BY:
Bill Russell, Beaver

Gardener's Special Platter

DIRECTIONS

On 12-inch glass serving plate, arrange zucchini with cauliflower and broccoli, alternating around the outside of the plate, placing stalks toward the outside. Cover and microwave for 9 minutes on high, or until vegetables are barely tender. Combine melted margarine, garlic salt and thyme. When vegetables are done, drain off excess liquid; arrange tomato wedges over vegetables. Drizzle butter mixture over vegetables and sprinkle with parmesan cheese. Microwave 1 to 2 minutes on high, uncovered, until tomatoes are heated.

NOTE

If zucchini is omitted, sprinkle vegetables with 1 tablespoon water before cooking.

INGREDIENTS

2 medium zucchini, sliced with skin on

1 1/2 pounds fresh broccoli, cut into small pieces

1/2 medium head cauliflower, cut into small flowerets

3 tablespoons margarine, melted

1/2 teaspoon garlic salt

1/4 teaspoon thyme

2 medium fresh tomato wedges

1/4 cup parmesan cheese

SUBMITTED BY:
Leila Welborn, Murrsyville

America's
HOME COOKING

Great Aunt Margaret Tarr's Cheesy Vegetables

DIRECTIONS

Precook vegetables for 3 to 5 minutes. While vegetables cook, make a cheese sauce by melting butter, adding flour, stirring to make a paste and adding milk. Cook sauce, stirring constantly, until thick. Add cubed cheese, a little at a time, stirring until smooth. Do not scorch. If sauce becomes too thick, thin with milk. Place drained vegetables into a casserole dish or slow cooker (on low) and heat until all flavors have mixed together.

NOTE

Any veggies can be added to the cauliflower. This recipe can be made ahead of time, just add cheese sauce when ready to heat.

INGREDIENTS

2 (16-ounce) packages froz
cauliflower florets

1 (16-ounce) package froze
peas

1 (16-ounce) package
frozen lima beans or other
vegetable of choice

2 tablespoons butter

2 tablespoons flour

1 1/4 cup milk (plus more
to thin sauce)

1 pound pasteurized proce
cheese, cubed

SUBMITTED BY:
Linda Pipp, Fredericktown

America's
HOME COOKING

Italian Green Beans

DIRECTIONS

Cook sausage with the onion and garlic until cooked through and no pink remains. Mix with all the remaining ingredients and place in a large slow cooker on low. Cook for 8 hours or until beans are cooked to taste.

NOTE

For a thicker sauce, simmer recipe on the stove for about 1 1/2 hours instead of using the slow cooker.

INGREDIENTS

1 pound hot or mild bulk Italian sausage

1 small onion, chopped

2 cloves garlic, minced

1 (28-ounce) can tomato puree

1 (15-ounce) can diced tomatoes, drained

1 tablespoon chopped fresh parsley

1 teaspoon dried sweet basil or 1 tablespoon fresh

Dash of oregano

1/2 cup grated romano cheese

2 pounds fresh green beans

SUBMITTED BY:
Diane Verdish, White Oak

America's
HOME COOKING

Leeks with Olive Oil (a la Turk)

DIRECTIONS

Clean the leeks thoroughly by slicing the leaves lengthwise and running them under the faucet for a few minutes. Clean and peel carrots. Cut the carrots and leeks into 1/4-inch-long round pieces. Fry leeks and carrots lightly in olive oil for a few minutes. Add rice, water, sugar, salt and pepper. Close lid of pot and simmer for 35 to 45 minutes, until rice is cooked. Let sit for 10 minutes and transfer into serving bowl. Cover and cool in the refrigerator for 1 to 2 hours. Serve cold with a lemon quarter on the side of the plate. Serves 4.

INGREDIENTS

4 stalks leek with white stems at least 4 inches long

2 medium carrots

4 ounces olive oil

2 ounces rice

8 ounces water

Sugar

Salt and pepper

1 lemon, quartered, for serving

SUBMITTED BY:
Omar Akin

Mom's Zucchini Casserole

DIRECTIONS

Preheat oven to 350 degrees. Spray a rectangular baking dish with cooking spray or grease the bottom with butter or oil. Layer zucchini on the bottom, followed by a layer of tomatoes and then the cheese slices. Sprinkle vegetables and cheese with breadcrumbs and then lightly sprinkle seasonings. Repeat layers until the top of the baking dish is reached or vegetables are used up. Sprinkle parsley on top. Bake, covered with aluminum foil, for 30 minutes. Remove foil and bake an additional 10 to 15 minutes or until cooked through.

INGREDIENTS

2 large zucchini, sliced about 1/4 inch thick

3 large tomatoes, sliced about 1/4 inch thick

16 ounces mozzarella cheese, sliced

2 cups breadcrumbs

Garlic powder, to taste

Onion powder, to taste

Celery salt, to taste

Salt and pepper, to taste

Parsley

SUBMITTED BY:
Karen Lee Puchnick, Butler

America's
HOME COOKING

Nanna's Eggplant Patties

DIRECTIONS

Cut unpeeled eggplant into small cubes, steam until tender. Drain, cool and squeeze water out. Combine with all other ingredients, mix well and form into small patties. Fry in vegetable or olive oil until golden brown.

NOTE

These patties are also known as vegetarian burgers or black cookies.

INGREDIENTS

1 large eggplant (about 2 pounds)

1/2 cup fresh basil, chopped

1 cup breadcrumbs

1/2 teaspoon salt

1/4 teaspoon pepper

1/4 teaspoon garlic powder

1/2 cup grated parmesan cheese

1 large egg, beaten

SUBMITTED BY:
Marianne Cascone-Hilty, Arnold

Onions Oliver

DIRECTIONS

Peel onions, but leave whole. Parboil onions in 2 quarts of salted simmering water for 5 minutes. Remove, drain and cool. Preheat oven to 350 degrees. Slice onion on the root end just enough to create a flat surface to allow bulb to stand upright. From the cut on the bottom, measure approximately the width of a slice of bacon to the top. Cut the top off at that line, but reserve top. Using a melon baller, or a teaspoon, hollow out the center of onion, leaving about 3 to 4 layers of skin (depending on the size and maturity of onions). Reserve the onion cores. Strip each rosemary sprig approximately 2 inches from stem end. Reserve stripped leaves. Wrap 1 piece of bacon around each onion bowl and secure it to the onion with the partially stripped rosemary stem. Set wrapped bowls aside in an ovenproof baking dish. On a cutting board, finely dice onion cores, tops and reserved rosemary leaves. Place mixture in a mixing bowl and add olive oil, cream and about 3/4 cup parmesan cheese. Season with salt and pepper, to taste. Using a teaspoon, fill each onion bowl with the cheese and onion mixture, mounding it slightly over the top. Place each onion bowl back into the baking dish and sprinkle with remaining parmesan cheese. Bake for about 30 minutes or until bacon is crisp.

INGREDIENTS

6 whole medium white or yellow onions

6 sprigs rosemary

6 strips bacon, cut thick

1/4 cup olive oil

1/4 cup heavy cream

1 cup shredded parmesan cheese

Salt and pepper, to taste

SUBMITTED BY:
John Messner, Moon Township

162

Stuffed Artichokes

DIRECTIONS

Choose artichokes that are heavy for their size with no purple leaves. The artichokes' leaves should be slightly closed. Wash and clean artichokes by cutting off the bottom stem and clipping off the top "pinchy" ends. Remove any tough leaves and rinse thoroughly. Mix all ingredients except olive oil. Stuff as much of the breadcrumb mixture as possible down into the artichoke layers all the way around. Place into a heavy pot. Drizzle the top of the artichokes liberally with olive oil. Add 1/4 inch of water to the pot, cover and steam on low heat for approximately 45 minutes or until the leaves peel off easily. To eat, pull off individual leaves and scrape off the stuffing and tender bottom part of the leaves with front teeth. When the prickly inner leaves are reached, remove them, as well as the thistle part of the artichoke, and enjoy the fleshy bottom, or heart, with a fork.

INGREDIENTS

4 nice-sized artichokes

1 cup fine breadcrumbs

1/4 cup romano cheese, grated

1/4 cup fresh parsley, chopped

Salt and pepper, to taste

Olive oil

SUBMITTED BY:
Amy Thumpston, Jennifer McGowan and Betsy Winters

Sweet and Sour Green Beans

DIRECTIONS

Leave bacon as a large slab and slice in opposite direction of bacon slices, making 1/2-inch square pieces. (Bacon cuts easier when partially frozen.) Separate the pieces and place in large frying pan. Cook bacon until slightly browned at medium-high flame and then add onion rings. Cook mixture until the bacon is very crispy and onions are slightly browned, limp and translucent, about 20 to 25 minutes. Stir mixture frequently. (Onion/bacon mixture will be dark.) Take off flame for a few minutes and stir in vinegar and sugar. Add mixture to green beans and carefully mix so green beans are not mashed. Place in oven, covered, at 325 degrees for about 20 minutes or until hot. Mix and serve.

INGREDIENTS

1 pound regular-sliced bacon

1 very large yellow onion, cut into thick slices

1/2 cup white vinegar

4 rounded tablespoons sugar

2 (14 1/2-ounce) cans fresh-cut green beans, drained

NOTE

Do not drain bacon and onion mixture. It can be made up a day ahead and then refrigerated. Just heat mixture to obtain mixable consistency and then add to green beans. Finish heating as noted above.

SUBMITTED BY:
Lori Walter, West View

Vegetable Bake

DIRECTIONS

Preheat oven to 350 degrees. Mix green beans through onion well and put into a greased 9x13-inch baking dish. Mix bread-crumbs and melted butter together for topping. Top green bean mixture with buttered breadcrumbs. Bake for 20 minutes or until breadcrumbs are brown.

INGREDIENTS

1 (10 1/2-ounce) can French-cut green beans, drained

1 (10 1/2-ounce) can whole kernel corn

1/2 cup mayonnaise

1/2 cup shredded sharp cheese

1/2 cup chopped green pepper

2 tablespoons chopped onion

2 cups breadcrumbs

1/2 cup (1 stick) butter or margarine, melted

SUBMITTED BY:
Catherine Monte Carlo, Monongahela

FAMILY FAVORITES

Desserts and Sweets

7 Up Pound Cake

DIRECTIONS

Preheat oven to 350 degrees. Grease and flour a tube pan. Add lemon and vanilla extracts to 7 Up. Cream butter and sugar in a mixer for 5 minutes. Add 1 egg at a time, beating thoroughly after each addition. Add 1 cup flour and beat; add 1/3 cup of 7 Up and beat. Alternate flour and 7 Up ending with flour. Pour batter into tube pan and bake for 45 to 50 minutes.

NOTE

All refrigerated ingredients must be at room temperature.

INGREDIENTS

1 teaspoon lemon extract

1 teaspoon vanilla extract

1 cup 7 Up

1 1/2 cups (3 sticks) butter substitute

3 cups sugar

5 eggs

3 cups presifted flour

SUBMITTED BY:
Marion Stewart, Pittsburgh

America's
HOME COOKING

Anise Cakes

DIRECTIONS

Mix ingredients thoroughly and chill well. Roll dough out and cut out with a round, diamond or star cookie cutter. Place on a lightly floured cloth and let dry overnight. The next day, bake at 350 degrees for 10 minutes on lightly greased cookie sheets.

INGREDIENTS

3 1/2 cups flour

2 1/4 cups sugar

5 eggs

1/8 cup (1 ounce) butter

1 teaspoon baking powder, dissolved in a little milk

1/2 teaspoon anise oil

SUBMITTED BY:

Peg Bittner, South Park

169

Apple Pie in a Bag

DIRECTIONS

To make crust, mix flour, sugar and salt. Add the butter and mix until mixture is coarse. Then, add water until mixture forms a dough ball. Divide dough into 2 pieces, place in plastic wrap and refrigerate overnight, or for at least 2 hours.

Preheat oven to 375 degrees. Roll out bottom crust. Toss apples, sugar, cornstarch, lemon juice and spices. Fill pie shell and dot with butter. Brush edges with water. Roll out top crust, place on top of pie and pinch dough together. Slide pie into a brown paper bag and staple it shut. Bake for 50 minutes. Remove from oven and cut a large circle in the top of the bag. Return to oven to brown an additional 15 minutes.

NOTE

Be sure that the brown bag does not touch the heating element in the oven.

INGREDIENTS

CRUST:

2 cups flour

1/4 cup sugar

Pinch of salt

1 cup cold unsalted butter, cut into pieces

1/3 cup ice water

FILLING:

5 Granny Smith apples, cored and sliced

1/2 cup sugar

1 1/2 tablespoons cornstarch

1 teaspoon fresh lemon juice

1 teaspoon cinnamon

Pinch of salt

1/8 teaspoon nutmeg

1 1/2 tablespoons cold butter, cut into pieces

SUBMITTED BY:
Cay Welch, Blairsville

Apricot Lemon Marmalade

DIRECTIONS

Put water in saucepan and add apricots and sugar. Slice lemon into very thin slices and then dice into tiny pieces. Add to pot and stir. Cook slowly, uncovered, on medium heat for 30 minutes. Then, mash with potato masher, leaving some chunks. Stir and cook 15 minutes until thick. Cool, put in jars and store in refrigerator.

INGREDIENTS

4 cups water

8 ounces dried apricots

1/2 cup sugar

1/2 fresh lemon

SUBMITTED BY:

Patti Kozar, Corapolis

171

Baklava

DIRECTIONS

Mix syrup ingredients in a small pan on stove. Cook about 45 minutes or until it sticks to the side of a spoon. Do not overcook. Thaw pastry according to package directions. Mix walnuts and sugar. Brush the bottom of large sheet pan and begin layering 10 pieces of phyllo, brushing in between each layer. Then, spread on ground nuts and sugar mixture. Layer 10 more sheets, brushing with butter between layers. Brush the top with butter. Cool entire pan. Cut into diamonds and bake until golden in a 350-degree oven. Slowly pour slightly cooled syrup on baklava.

INGREDIENTS

1 (16-ounce) package phyllo dough

1 pound melted butter

1 pound ground walnuts, about 4 cups

1/2 cup sugar

SYRUP:

3 cups sugar

1 cup water

Juice from 1/2 fresh lemon

SUBMITTED BY:
Barbara Knezovich, McKeesport

172

Bishop's Bread

DIRECTIONS

Preheat oven to 325 degrees. Mix the dry ingredients. Add the nuts, dates, cherries and chocolate chips; toss lightly. Beat the eggs, sugar and vanilla. Stir into the dry ingredient and fruit mixture. Grease and flour a 9x5x3-inch loaf pan. Bake for 1 hour and 15 minutes, checking doneness with a toothpick after 1 hour. Turn bread out on a wire rack to cool. When totally cooled, wrap well and store for 1 or 2 days before slicing.

INGREDIENTS

2 cups all-purpose flour

2 teaspoons baking powder

1 teaspoon salt

1 cup chopped nuts, such as pecans

1 cup chopped dates

1 cup sliced maraschino cherries

1 cup semi-sweet chocolate pieces

4 large eggs, beaten

1 cup sugar

1 teaspoon vanilla

SUBMITTED BY:
Carol Corbett Blank, Pittsburgh

Black Magic Cake with Whipped Cream Icing

DIRECTIONS

Preheat oven to 350 degrees. Combine dry ingredients in large mixer bowl. Add eggs, coffee, buttermilk or sour milk, oil and vanilla. Beat at medium speed for 2 minutes (batter will be thin). Pour into greased and floured 13x9x2-inch pan or 2 9-inch cake pans. Bake for 35 to 40 minutes for oblong pan or 30 to 35 minutes for cake pans. Cool and frost with whipped cream icing.

To make icing, beat cream until slightly thick. Add chocolate syrup and beat until icing resembles cream.

INGREDIENTS

CAKE:

1 1/3 cups all-purpose flour

2 cups sugar

3/4 cups baking cocoa

2 teaspoons baking soda

1 teaspoon baking powder

1 teaspoon salt

1 teaspoon cinnamon

2 eggs

1 cup strong black coffee
(or 2 teaspoons instant coffee plus 1 cup boiling water)

1 cup buttermilk or sour milk

1/2 cup vegetable oil

1 teaspoon vanilla

ICING:

1 pint whipping cream

1 cup chocolate syrup

SUBMITTED BY:
Chris Novotny, Baden

America's
HOME COOKING

Black Walnut Cookies

DIRECTIONS

Mix all ingredients well. Form into logs
and wrap in wax paper. Chill thoroughly.
Preheat oven to 350 degrees. Slice logs and
bake on lightly greased cookie sheets for 8 to
10 minutes.

INGREDIENTS

2 eggs

2 cups brown sugar

1/2 cup butter, melted

3 cups flour

1 teaspoon baking soda

1 teaspoon baking powder

1 cup ground black walnuts

3/4 teaspoon vanilla

SUBMITTED BY:
Peg Bittner, South Park

America's
HOME COOKING

Brown Pudding

DIRECTIONS

Preheat oven to 350 degrees. Mix raisins through salt and put in a deep round or oval pan. Mix topping ingredients and pour on top of raisin mixture. Do not mix bottom and top together. Bake for about 40 minutes.

Raisin mixture on the bottom will thicken as it cooks while the mixture on top will become a cake. Spoon out a piece of cake and put some raisin mixture from bottom over the top of cake.

INGREDIENTS

1 cup raisins

1 cup brown sugar

4 cups hot water

2 tablespoons butter

Pinch of salt

TOPPING:

1 cup white sugar

2 tablespoons butter

1 cup sour milk (add 1 tablespoon vinegar to milk)

2 cups flour

2 teaspoons cinnamon

2 teaspoons nutmeg

2 teaspoons vanilla

2 teaspoons baking soda

SUBMITTED BY:
Barbara Crissman, Vandergrift

Butterscotch Pie

DIRECTIONS

Preheat oven to 350 degrees. Mix brown sugar and flour in a saucepan and add the water and egg yolks. Cook over a low heat until mixture thickens. Remove from heat and add vanilla and butter; blend thoroughly. Pour into a prepared pie shell. Beat the egg whites until stiff peaks form. Stir in sugar. Top pie with this mixture and cook in oven until egg whites are lightly browned.

INGREDIENTS

2 cups brown sugar, firmly packed

4 tablespoons flour

1 1/2 cups water

4 egg yolks, lightly beaten

1 teaspoon vanilla extract

1 teaspoon butter

Prepared pie shell, preferably graham cracker

Egg whites

2 teaspoons white sugar

SUBMITTED BY:
Sharon Morford, North Hills

Caramel Dumplings

DIRECTIONS

Mix batter ingredients and set aside. In a heavy skillet, over low heat, stir 1/2 cup sugar until it melts and turns light brown. Add water, butter and additional cup sugar. Stir until mixture comes to a low boil. Drop batter in caramel by spoonfuls. Cover and cook over very low heat for 15 to 20 minutes. Dumplings can be served with nuts and ice cream.

INGREDIENTS

BATTER:

1/2 cup milk

3 tablespoons butter

1 1/2 cups flour

1/2 cup sugar

2 teaspoon baking powder

1 teaspoon vanilla

CARAMEL:

1/2 cup sugar

2 cups boiling water

2 tablespoons butter

1 cup sugar

Nuts or ice cream, for serving

SUBMITTED BY:
Peggy Rae, Apollo

Carrot Cupcakes

DIRECTIONS

In a medium bowl, combine grated carrots and brown sugar. Set aside for 1 hour; then stir in raisins. Preheat oven to 350 degrees. Prepare 30 to 36 muffin pans with paper liners. In a large bowl, beat eggs until light and fluffy. Gradually beat in the white sugar, oil and vanilla. Stir in the pineapple. Combine the flour, baking soda, salt and cinnamon. Stir into the wet mixture until absorbed. Finally, stir in the carrot mixture and walnuts. Pour evenly into the prepared muffin liners. Bake for 25 to 30 minutes, until cupcake tests done with a toothpick. Cool for 10 minutes before removing from pan. When completely cooled, frost with cream cheese frosting.

To make frosting, beat cream cheese, butter and vanilla. Gradually add powdered sugar. Spread over cooled cupcakes and refrigerate until ready to serve.

INGREDIENTS

6 cups grated carrots

1 cup brown sugar

1 cup raisins

4 eggs

1 1/2 cups white sugar

1 cup vegetable oil

2 teaspoons vanilla extract

1 cup crushed pineapple, drained

3 cups all-purpose flour

1 1/2 teaspoons baking soda

1 teaspoon salt

4 teaspoons ground cinnamon

1 cup chopped walnuts

Frosting:

2 (8-ounce) packages cream cheese

1/2 cup (1 stick) butter

1 teaspoon vanilla

2 cups powdered sugar

SUBMITTED BY:
Karen Manni, Atlasburg

Cassava Cake

DIRECTIONS

Preheat oven to 350 degrees. Mix ingredients together and pour in lightly buttered 9-inch square pan. Bake for 40 to 45 minutes.

If desired, add 1 white or brown sugar to reserved coconut cream. Spread over baked cake and put under broiler for about 5 minutes, or until bubbly.

INGREDIENTS

1 pound frozen shredded cassava, thawed (available in Asian food stores)

1 (14-ounce) can coconut milk (reserve 1/4 cup of its thick cream)

1 1/4 cup sugar

2 eggs, lightly beaten

1/3 cup white or brown sugar, for topping (optional)

SUBMITTED BY:
Pepita Jacobs, Indiana

Cay's Killer Cheesecake

DIRECTIONS

Preheat oven to 500 degrees. Line a 9-inch springform pan with butter and pat with graham cracker crumbs. Mix the cheese, sugar, flour, lemon and orange zests, and vanilla until smooth. Add eggs, then yolks and finally the cream. Pour into springform pan and bake 10 minutes or until top of cake is golden. Reduce oven to 200 or 225 degrees and bake for 1 hour. Remove cake from oven. Cool until it reaches room temperature then remove side of the pan. Top with favorite topping.

INGREDIENTS

Butter

Graham cracker crumbs

2 1/2 pounds of cream cheese, softened to room temperature

1 3/4 cup granulated sugar

3 tablespoons all-purpose flour

Zest of 1 lemon

Zest of 1 orange

1/4 teaspoon vanilla

5 eggs

2 additional egg yolks

1/4 cup heavy whipping cream

SUBMITTED BY:
Cay Welch, Blairsville

America's
HOME COOKING

Cheesecake

DIRECTIONS

Combine crust ingredients and line the bottom of a 9-inch springform pan with this mixture. Preheat oven to 325 degrees. Combine all filling ingredients and beat at medium speed for 20 to 25 minutes. Pour mixture into the prepared pan. Bake for 40 minutes; cool for 35 minutes. Beat topping ingredients together for 10 minutes. Pour over top of baked and cooled cake. Bake at 400 degrees for 10 minutes. Watch cheesecake carefully; it should be only very slightly brown on top. Refrigerate overnight.

INGREDIENTS

CRUST:

26 finely crushed graham crackers

3/4 cup butter

1 tablespoon brown sugar

FILLING:

3 (8-ounce) packages cream cheese

4 eggs

1 cup sugar

1 teaspoon vanilla

TOPPING:

1 pint sour cream

3/4 cup sugar

SUBMITTED BY:
Nancy Polinsky, Squirrel Hill

America's
HOME COOKING

Chewy Chocolate Cookies

DIRECTIONS

Preheat oven to 375 degrees. Mix together butter and sugar until fluffy. Add eggs and vanilla; beat until well blended. Add dry ingredients just until blended. Drop by spoonfuls onto ungreased cookie sheet. Bake for 7 or 8 minutes. Makes about 4 1/2 dozen.

INGREDIENTS

1 1/4 cup (2 1/2 sticks) butter

2 cups sugar

2 eggs

1 teaspoon vanilla

1/2 teaspoon salt

1 teaspoon baking soda

2 cups flour

3/4 cup cocoa

SUBMITTED BY:
Melinda Roberts, Beaver

America's
HOME COOKING

Chocolate Cheesecake

DIRECTIONS

Preheat oven to 300 degrees. Pour all but 1 cup of the dry cake mix into a bowl. (Set aside remaining cup of mix). Add 1 egg and oil (mixture will be crumbly). Press into 9x13-inch cake pan. In the same mixing bowl, blend cream cheese and sugar thoroughly. Add 3 eggs and remaining cake mix. Beat for 1 minute at medium speed. Add milk and vanilla. Mix until smooth. Pour into prepared crust. Bake for 55 to 65 minutes, until set. When very cool, spread cheesecake with whipped topping, making a design if desired. Garnish with chocolate sprinkles; chill.

NOTE

For chocoholics: before putting on the whipped topping, fold the dry chocolate drink mix into the whipped topping and spread on cheesecake. Chill.

INGREDIENTS

1 (18 1/4-ounce) box moist chocolate cake mix (mix should include pudding)

4 eggs

1 tablespoon oil

2 (8-ounce) packages cream cheese

1/2 cup sugar

1 1/2 cups milk

1 teaspoon vanilla

1 (12-ounce) container whipped topping

Chocolate sprinkles, for garnishing (optional)

7 ounces dry chocolate drink mix (optional)

SUBMITTED BY:
Edwynna Roach, Russellton

America's HOME COOKING

Chocolate Chippers

DIRECTIONS

Preheat oven to 350 degrees. Cream shortening, sugars, egg and vanilla until fluffy. Sift dry ingredients. Blend into creamed mixture. Stir in chocolate chips and nuts. Drop by teaspoon on a greased cookie sheet. Bake for 10 to 12 minutes.

INGREDIENTS

1/2 cup shortening

1/2 cup sugar

1/4 cup brown sugar

1 egg

1 teaspoon vanilla

1 cup flour

1/2 teaspoon baking soda

3/4 teaspoon salt

1 cup chocolate chips

1/2 cup walnuts, chopped

SUBMITTED BY:
Joyce Cress, Morgantown

Chocolate Feather Pudding

DIRECTIONS

Beat egg until light and fluffy. Beat in sugar and stir in milk. Sift dry ingredients together and add to mixture. Add melted chocolate and mix thoroughly. Pour into well-greased mold and steam for 2 hours. To make hard sauce, thoroughly mix all 3 sauce ingredients together. Chill for at least 1 hour before serving. Serve pudding with hard sauce.

INGREDIENTS

1 egg

1 cup sugar

1 cup milk

1 1/2 cups bread flour

2 teaspoons baking powder

1/4 teaspoon salt

1 1/2 squares bitter chocolate, melted

HARD SAUCE:

1/2 cup soft butter

1 cup confectioners sugar

2 teaspoons vanilla

SUBMITTED BY:
Fran Borrebach, Bradford Woods

186

Co-Co Cappuccino Cheesecake

DIRECTIONS

Preheat oven to 325 degrees. In a mixing bowl, combine cake mix, butter, egg and coffee granules, using hands to combine smoothly. Press onto bottom and sides of a greased 10-inch springform pan. In a mixing bowl, beat cream cheese until smooth. Beat in milk and chocolate chips. Dissolve coffee granules in hot water. Add coffee and eggs to cream cheese mixture. Beat on low speed until smooth. Pour into crust. Place pan on a baking sheet. Bake for 50 to 55 minutes or until center is set. Cool on wire rack for 10 minutes. Carefully run a knife around edges to loosen. Cool 1 hour longer. Chill overnight. Remove sides of pan; place onto a plate. Mix whipped topping with almond extract. Top cheesecake with almond-flavored whipping topping mixture. Garnish with slivered toasted almonds. Chill until ready to serve. Makes 12 to 16 servings.

INGREDIENTS

CRUST:

1 (18 1/4-ounce) package devil's food cake mix

6 tablespoons butter or margarine, melted

1 egg

1 to 3 tablespoons instant coffee granules

FILLING:

2 (8-ounce) packages light cream cheese, softened

1 (14-ounce) can sweetened condensed milk

2 cups (1 12-ounce package) semi-sweet chocolate chips, melted

3 to 6 tablespoons instant coffee granules

1/4 cup hot water

3 eggs, lightly beaten

1 cup light whipped topping

1/2 teaspoon almond extract

1/4 cup slivered almonds, toasted, for garnishing

SUBMITTED BY:
Rosemarie Weleski, Natrona Heights

Coconut Macaroons

DIRECTIONS

Preheat oven to 350 degrees. In large mixing bowl, combine coconut, sweetened condensed milk and extracts; mix well. Drop by rounded teaspoonfuls onto aluminum foil-lined and generously greased baking sheets. Bake 8 to 10 minutes or until lightly browned around the edges. Immediately remove from baking sheets. Store loosely covered at room temperature.

INGREDIENTS

5 1/2 cups flaked coconut

1 (14-ounce) can sweetened condensed milk

2 teaspoons vanilla extract

1 1/2 teaspoons almond extract

SUBMITTED BY:
Jessica Manni, Johnstown

188

Cranberry Pistachio Biscotti

DIRECTIONS

Preheat oven to 350 degrees. Mix oil and sugar; add vanilla extract and almond flavoring. Add eggs. Combine all dry ingredients separately. Add cranberries and nuts to dry ingredients; then add egg mixture. Divide dough in half (with water-moistened fingers). Make 2 12-inch logs and place logs on parchment paper-lined cookie sheet. Bake for 35 minutes, remove from oven and reduce oven temperature to 275 degrees. Cut dough diagonally (making approximately 14 cookies from each log) and place in oven for 8 minutes.

INGREDIENTS

1/4 cup olive oil

3/4 cup granulated sugar

2 teaspoons vanilla extract

1/4 teaspoon almond flavoring

2 eggs

1 3/4 cup flour

1/4 teaspoon salt

1/4 teaspoon baking powder

1/2 cup dried cranberries

1 1/2 cup shelled pistachios

SUBMITTED BY:
Toni Bell, Squirrel Hill

America's HOME COOKING

189

Danish Apple Pastry

DIRECTIONS

Preheat oven to 400 degrees (or 350 degrees if using a glass dish). Mix all dry ingredients except corn flakes. Add shortening and cut into flour. Put yolk into a measuring cup and add milk to equal 2/3 cup. Add to shortening and flour and mix well. Divide dough into 2 pieces. Place 1 piece into an 11x14-inch pan. Sprinkle dough with corn flakes and add apples. Add sugar and cinnamon mixture. Roll second piece of dough and place on top of apples. Prick with fork or make small cuts in dough. Slightly beat egg white and brush on top of dough. Bake for 1 hour. If pastry browns too quickly, cover with foil. Beat all ingredients for frosting together. Drizzle frosting on pastry immediately after removing from oven.

INGREDIENTS

2 1/2 cups flour

1 teaspoon salt

1 cup shortening

1 egg yolk

2/3 cup milk, scant

2 cups corn flakes, crushed

8 to 10 sliced Macintosh or Granny Smith apples

1 cup sugar mixed with 1 teaspoon cinnamon

FROSTING:

1 cup powdered sugar

1 tablespoon milk

1 teaspoon vanilla

SUBMITTED BY:
An'ge Ross Sassos, Greensburg

Fruit and Coconut Dessert Dumplings

DIRECTIONS

Place neufchatel cheese into a mixing bowl. Fork through cheese to soften it slightly. Add shredded coconut, honey and vanilla. Fork through to combine ingredients. (If cheese mixture is too hard, microwave for 10 seconds.) Using a butter knife, spread approximately 1 1/2 teaspoons of cheese mixture onto middle of each wonton wrapper. Add frozen fruit; 1 piece of either the mango or the pineapple or 2 to 3 blueberries. Apply water to 2 edges of the wonton wrapper, fold two corners together and crimp sides completely. Repeat until all the cheese mixture is used, about 30 dumplings. Heat oil in saucepan over medium-high heat. Line a plate with paper towels for draining. When oil is hot, drop dumplings into oil one by one and cook until dumpling floats and expands, about 5 seconds. Remove from oil and drain. After each dumpling has drained, sprinkle generously with sugar. Serve hot or cool.

NOTE

This recipe can be partly prepared in advance. Follow recipe directions through filling dumplings. Wrap filled dumplings individually in plastic wrap and store in fridge until ready to fry.

INGREDIENTS

1 (8-ounce) package organic neufchatel cheese

1/2 cup organic shredded coconut

1/4 cup tupelo honey

2 teaspoons vanilla extrac

1 (12-ounce) package wonton wrappers

1 1/2 cup frozen mango chunks

1 1/2 cup frozen pineapple chunks

1 cup frozen blueberries

Water, for sealing wonton

Vegetable oil, for deep frying

Sugar shaker, for finishing

SUBMITTED BY:

Mose, Jennifer and Isis Berymon, Mt. Oliver

Fudge Crackles

DIRECTIONS

Preheat oven to 300 degrees. Mix flour, baking powder and salt. In a heavy saucepan, stir butter and chocolate over low heat until smooth and melted; cool. Stir in 1 cup of sugar, eggs, vanilla and nuts until well blended. Stir in flour mixture until blended. Cover and chill 1 1/2 to 2 hours until dough is firm enough to shape. Roll into 1 1/2-inch balls; roll balls in the remaining 3 tablespoons sugar. Place balls 2 inches apart on ungreased cookie sheet. Bake for about 20 minutes until crackled on top and slightly firm to touch. Remove immediately to rack to cool. Makes about 2 dozen cookies.

INGREDIENTS

1 cup flour

1 teaspoon baking powder

1/4 teaspoon salt

1/4 cup (1/2 stick) butter

3 (1-ounce) squares unsweetened chocolate

1 cup plus 3 tablespoons sugar

2 eggs

1 teaspoon vanilla

1/2 cup chopped nuts

SUBMITTED BY:
Dolores Thorp, Salineville

Gram's Gingerbread Men

DIRECTIONS

Preheat oven to 350 degrees. Combine pudding, butter and sugar. Cream thoroughly. Blend in egg and combine remaining ingredients. Blend all until creamy. Chill until firm. Roll on slightly floured board to about 1/8 inch thick. Cut with cookie cutter. Bake for 10 to 12 minutes. Decorate with tinted icing as desired.

INGREDIENTS

1 (4-ounce) package butterscotch pudding

1/2 cup (1 stick) butter

1/2 cup firmly packed brown sugar

1 egg

1 1/2 cups sifted flour

1 1/2 teaspoons ginger

1/2 teaspoon cinnamon

1/2 teaspoon baking soda

SUBMITTED BY:
Amy Thumpston, Jennifer McGowan and Betsy Winters

Grandma's Apple Butter Pie

DIRECTIONS

Preheat oven to 350 degrees. Blend all ingredients well and pour into 1 unbaked crust. With the second crust, make the lattice top by cutting strips and interweaving them. Be sure to crimp lattice firmly to the bottom crust. Bake for 45 minutes. Let cool completely before serving.

INGREDIENTS

1 cup apple butter

1 cup water

1 rounded tablespoon cornstarch

2 tablespoons granulated sugar

1 rounded teaspoon cinnamon

2 prepared homemade pie crusts

SUBMITTED BY:
Denean Y. Ross, Pittsburgh

America's
HOME COOKING

Grandma's Nut Rolls

DIRECTIONS

Cut flour, salt, sugar and shortening as if for a pie. Add sour cream. Cut into flour mixture and set aside. In a separate bowl, mix together the yeast, warm water and sugar. Let rest awhile until bubbly. Fold in egg yolks and vanilla. Stir together and pour wet ingredients into flour mixture. Work all ingredients until well blended. Form into 5 balls, place on pan and cover with wax paper and tea towel. Refrigerate overnight. Preheat oven to 350 degrees. With a rolling pin, roll out one ball of dough in powdered sugar. Roll dough in the shape of a rectangle, approximately 10x14 inches. Mix together nut filling ingredients. Evenly spread 1/5 of the nut mixture onto dough. Roll filled dough from the 14-inch side. Prick top of roll with fork in 4 or 5 places. Place on a greased cookie sheet. Bake for 30 minutes. When cooled, wrap tightly in aluminum foil.

INGREDIENTS

5 cups flour

1/2 teaspoon salt

1/2 cup sugar

1 cup butter flavor shortening

1 cup sour cream

2 packages dry yeast

1/4 cup warm water

1/2 teaspoon sugar

4 egg yolks

1 teaspoon vanilla

Powdered sugar

NUT FILLING:

4 egg whites, beaten until foamy

1 teaspoon vanilla

5 cups ground walnuts

1 1/2 cups granulated sugar

1/2 teaspoon salt

1/2 teaspoon cinnamon

SUBMITTED BY:
Rosalie Frenchak, Butler

America's
HOME COOKING

195

Grossmutter's Schmerkase Pie

DIRECTIONS

Preheat oven to 350 degrees. Prepare pastry shell. Beat eggs until light. Add sugar gradually; beat well. Add salt, cream, cottage cheese, flour, lemon juice and lemon rind. Mix well and pour into unbaked pastry shell. Combine sugar and cinnamon; mix well. Sprinkle sugar/cinnamon mixture over top of pie. Bake for 40 minutes or until knife inserted near center comes out clean.

INGREDIENTS

1 9-inch unbaked pie shell

3 eggs

1/2 cup granulated sugar

1/8 teaspoon salt

1/2 cup light cream

2 cups cottage cheese

2 tablespoons flour

2 tablespoons fresh lemon juice

1 teaspoon grated lemon rind

TOPPING:

2 tablespoons sugar

1/2 teaspoon cinnamon

SUBMITTED BY:
Barbara Lanke, Woods Run
(North Side)

Honeyed Applesauce

DIRECTIONS

Place all ingredients in a large saucepan. Cover and bring to a boil. Reduce heat and simmer 8 to 10 minutes or until apples are tender. Mash lightly and let cool. If necessary, add sugar to taste. Makes 8 servings.

INGREDIENTS

8 Jonathan, Winesap or Macintosh apples, peeled, cored and diced

1/2 cup water

1 tablespoon honey

1 tablespoon lemon juice

Sugar, to taste (optional)

SUBMITTED BY:
Susan Cohen, Pittsburgh

Key Lime Pie

DIRECTIONS

Preheat oven to 350 degrees. Crush graham crackers into crumbs in a food processor. Melt the butter and mix it into the crumbs. Press the mixture into an 8-inch pie or tart pan and bake for 5 minutes. Remove the crust from the oven, but leave oven on. While the crust is baking, make the filling. Mix all ingredients together and pour mixture into the crust. Bake for 6 to 8 minutes, until moderately set. Remove the pie and increase heat to 400 degrees. While the pie is baking, make topping. Start beating the egg whites on low speed and gradually increase to high speed. Add the 1/4 teaspoon lemon juice or cream of tartar after 20 seconds. Add sugar very slowly, in a thin stream. Slather or pipe the meringue on top of the pie. Bake for 3 to 5 minutes until meringue is nicely brown. Let the pie cool to room temperature. Refrigerate, uncovered, for at least 4 hours before serving.

SUBMITTED BY:
Scott Pavelle, Ross Township

INGREDIENTS

CRUST:

1 1/4 (1 package) cups cinnamon graham crackers, crushed

1/3 cup unsalted butter, melted

FILLING:

3 egg yolks

1 (14-ounce) can sweetened condensed milk

1/2 cup plus 2 tablespoons fresh key lime or regular lime juice or a 50/50 mix of lemon and regular lime juice

2 teaspoons grated lime zest

TOPPING:

3 egg whites

1/4 teaspoon cream of tartar or lime juice

1/2 cup sugar

Killarney Bread

DIRECTIONS

Preheat oven to 350 degrees. Cream margarine, sugar and eggs. Sift flour, baking powder, baking soda and salt. Mix sour cream and vanilla until smooth. Add sour cream mixture along with flour mixture to creamed ingredients. Mix all topping ingredients together until incorporated. Grease and flour 2 loaf pans. Put 1/4 of the batter in each pan. Sprinkle with 1/4 of the topping mixture. Spread remaining batter into pan on top of topping carefully so as not to mix the topping into the batter. Sprinkle with remaining topping. Bake for 1 hour.

INGREDIENTS

BATTER:

1 cup margarine or butter

2 cups white sugar

4 eggs

4 cups flour

2 teaspoons baking powder

2 teaspoons baking soda

1 teaspoon salt

1 (16-ounce) carton sour cream

2 teaspoons vanilla

TOPPING:

1/2 cup white sugar

1/2 cup brown sugar

1 teaspoon cinnamon

1 cup chopped walnuts (optional)

SUBMITTED BY:
Connie Black, Ross Township

Lemon Zucchini Bread

DIRECTIONS

Preheat oven to 350 degrees. Beat eggs, sugar and oil until well mixed. Add lemon rind, lemon juice, lemon flavoring and food coloring (if using) and mix. Add zucchini and lemon pudding; mix well. Sift flour, salt, baking soda and baking powder together and add to the rest of the mixture. Mix well; then add coconut and nuts. Grease and flour 2 large or 3 medium loaf pans. Bake for 1 hour for large loaf pan and 45 minutes for medium pans. When cool, sprinkle top with powdered sugar.

INGREDIENTS

3 eggs

1 1/2 cups sugar

1 cup oil

Rind of 1 lemon, grated

Juice from 1 lemon

3 teaspoons lemon flavoring

Yellow food coloring (optional)

2 cups grated zucchini

1 (3-ounce) box instant lemon pudding

3 1/4 cups all-purpose flour

1 teaspoon salt

1 teaspoon baking soda

1/2 teaspoon baking powder

1/2 cup coconut

1/2 cup chopped nuts

Powdered sugar, for garnishing

SUBMITTED BY:
Sue Hoover, Finleyville

America's
HOME COOKING

Mandel Bread

DIRECTIONS

Preheat oven to 350 degrees. Beat eggs; add sugar and beat again. Add oil and beat. Add extracts and then mix baking powder and cinnamon into flour. Mix flour into batter 1 cup at a time; then add nuts and mix well. Make either 2 1/2 long loaves or 3 short ones, depending on the size of cookie sheets. Take dough, divide and make into long roll and put on long cookie sheet. Make rolls about 2 inches wide and shape square and even down the sides. Make a row down the middle of cookie sheet, reaching about half way. (If using short cookie sheets, make 3 loaves.) Bake for 25 minutes. Slice loaves diagonally and turn on side. Brown 5 to 10 minutes, turn over and brown opposite side. Do not over-brown bread.

INGREDIENTS

3 eggs

1 cup sugar

1 cup oil

1 teaspoon lemon extract

1 teaspoon almond extract

1 teaspoon baking powder

1 teaspoon cinnamon

3 cups flour

1 cup nuts, coarsely chopped

VARIATION

Leave out cinnamon, extracts and nuts. Instead, add 1 tablespoon orange zest and a cup of diced dried cranberries and 1/4 teaspoon salt.

SUBMITTED BY:
Barbara Heyman, Conway

America's
HOME COOKING

Mint Chocolate Angel Food Cake

DIRECTIONS

Preheat oven to 375 degrees. Into a bowl, sift together the flour, cocoa powder, 1/4 teaspoon of salt and 3/4 cup sugar. In another bowl, beat the whites with an electric mixer until they hold soft peaks; add the cream of tartar and remaining 1/4 teaspoon salt. Beat in remaining 3/4 cup sugar, a little at a time, beating until the whites hold stiff peaks. Fold in peppermint extract and the flour mixture, 1/4 cup at a time. Pour the batter into an ungreased 14x10-inch tube pan with a removable bottom and run a knife through it to remove any air bubbles. Bake the cake in the middle of oven for 35 to 40 minutes, or until a tester comes out clean. Invert the pan on a work surface and let the cake cool in the pan completely. Run a thin knife around the edge of the pan and remove the side. Run the knife under the bottom of the cake and around the tube to loosen the cake and invert the cake onto a plate.

INGREDIENTS

1 cup cake flour
(not self-rising)

1/2 cup unsweetened
cocoa powder

1/2 teaspoon salt

1 1/2 cups superfine
granulated sugar

10 large egg whites

1 1/2 teaspoons cream
of tartar

2/3 teaspoon peppermint
extract

SUBMITTED BY:
Elsie Henderson,
Wilkinsburg

Molasses Sugar Cookies

DIRECTIONS

Preheat oven to 375 degrees. Melt shortening in a 3- or 4-quart saucepan over low heat. Remove from heat and allow to cool. Add sugar, molasses and egg; beat well. Sift together flour, baking soda, spices and salt; add these to first mixture. Mix well and chill thoroughly. Form into 1-inch balls; roll in granulated sugar and place on greased cookie sheets 2 inches apart. Bake for 8 to 10 minutes. Makes 4 dozen cookies.

INGREDIENTS

3/4 cup shortening

1 cup sugar

1/4 cup molasses

1 egg

2 cups flour

2 teaspoons baking soda

1/2 teaspoon cloves

1/2 teaspoon ginger

1 teaspoon cinnamon

1/2 teaspoon salt

SUBMITTED BY:
Peg Bittner, South Park

Ninety-Minute Dinner Rolls

DIRECTIONS

Mix warm water, sugar and yeast. Let sit until bubbly. Heat milk and margarine. Gradually add wet ingredients to 1 cup flour and the dry ingredients and beat until smooth. Add 1 cup flour. Beat at high speed for 2 minutes. Stir in additional flour to make a soft dough. On floured board, knead 2 to 3 minutes. Divide dough into 12 equal pieces and shape into balls. Place in greased 8-inch round pan. Pour a 1 inch depth of boiling water into a large pan on the bottom rack of a cold oven. Set rolls on rack above water and cover. Close oven door. Let rolls rise for 30 minutes. Uncover rolls and remove pan of water. Turn oven to 375 degrees and bake 20 to 25 minutes or until done. Remove from pan to cool slightly. Serve warm.

INGREDIENTS

1/4 cup warm water

2 tablespoons sugar

1 package dry yeast

1/2 cup milk

2 tablespoons margarine

2 to 2 1/2 cups unsifted flour

1/2 teaspoon salt

SUBMITTED BY:
Virginia Jakub, Nottingham Township

204

Noodle Pudding

DIRECTIONS

Preheat oven to 350 degrees. Mix margarine through raisins together. Add noodles last. Put mixture in a greased pan. Mix topping ingredients. Place topping on mixture and bake for 1 hour.

INGREDIENTS

3/4 stick margarine

1 (3-ounce) package cream cheese

1/2 cup sugar

3 eggs

1 cup milk

1 cup apricot nectar

Raisins

1/2 pound medium noodles, boiled

TOPPING:

2 cups corn flake crumbs

6 tablespoons (3/4 stick) margarine, cut into dots

1/4 cup sugar

1 teaspoon cinnamon

SUBMITTED BY:
Carol Shrut, Bridgeville

America's
HOME COOKING

Palachinka
(Croatian Crepes)

DIRECTIONS

Mix all crepe ingredients together and beat well. Let batter stand in refrigerator overnight. The next day, mix batter well and fry thin pancakes (each about 1/4 cup batter). Combine filling ingredients and place a small amount of filling on each prepared pancake and roll up. Line rolled crepes in a baking pan; dot with butter or rub melted butter on top. Spread sour cream on top. Bake at 350 degrees until well warmed.

INGREDIENTS

CREPES:

1 1/4 cup flour

Pinch of salt

3 eggs, beaten

1 1/2 cups regular milk

2 to 3 tablespoons melted butter

2 tablespoons sugar

Cooking oil, for frying crepes

FILLING:

Ground nuts with honey or preserves

1 (8-ounce) package cream cheese

Ricotta cheese

2 eggs

Sugar, to taste

Butter

1 (16-ounce) container sour cream

SUBMITTED BY:
Mary Kocian and Josephine Kocian Crame, Reserve

Peanut Butter Pie

DIRECTIONS

Mix together cream cheese and powdered sugar. Add peanut butter and vanilla and mix until thoroughly blended. Fold in whipped topping. Spoon into pie crust. Chop 1/2 bag mini peanut butter cups into chunks and sprinkle on top of pie. Drizzle with chocolate syrup and refrigerate at least 4 hours.

INGREDIENTS

1 (8-ounce) package cream cheese, softened

1/2 cup powdered sugar

1/2 cup peanut butter, crunchy or smooth

1 teaspoon vanilla

1 (8-ounce) container whipped topping

1 ready-made sandwich-cookie pie crust

1 (10-ounce) bag miniature peanut butter cups

Chocolate syrup (optional)

SUBMITTED BY:
Amy Poston, Butler

America's
HOME COOKING

Pignoli Cookies

DIRECTIONS

Preheat oven to 325 degrees. Line cookie sheet with aluminum foil and grease or spray with cooking spray. Place pine nuts in a shallow pan. In a medium bowl beat paste, sugar, egg whites and lemon rind with an electric mixer until smooth. With slightly wet hands, form dough into 1-inch balls. Roll balls in the nuts and flatten slightly. Place 1 inch apart on the baking sheet. Bake 22 to 25 minutes until light gold. Cool for 5 minutes on the pan and then remove to a rack. Store tightly covered.

NOTE

The dough is easier to handle if refrigerated for 1 hour or so before forming and rolling in nuts.

INGREDIENTS

1 cup pine nuts

1 (8-ounce) can almond paste, cut in small pieces

2/3 cup sugar

2 egg whites

1 teaspoon grated lemon rind

SUBMITTED BY:
Chris Fennimore, "QED Cooks"

208

Polish Pound Cake

DIRECTIONS

Preheat oven to 300 degrees. Cream shortening, margarine and sugar together in a large mixing bowl. Add salt, evaporated milk and butternut flavoring. Add eggs, one at a time, beating after each addition. Slowly add flour. Add cherries (pat dry and sprinkle with flour before adding them to the batter) and nuts. Pour batter into a greased and floured bundt pan. Bake for 2 hours or until toothpick comes out clean. Cool and turn onto a cake plate. Sprinkle with confectionary sugar or glaze.

To make glaze, combine boiling water, butter and cherry juice. Mix well. Drizzle over cake.

INGREDIENTS

1/2 cup white shortening

1 cup (2 sticks) soft margarine

3 cups white sugar

1/4 teaspoon salt

1 cup evaporated milk

2 tablespoons butternut vanilla butternut flavoring

5 eggs

3 cups flour

1 (10-ounce) jar of maraschino cherries, drained

1 cup pecans or walnuts, chopped

Confectionary sugar

GLAZE:

3 tablespoons boiling water

1 tablespoon butter, melted

2 tablespoons cherry juice

SUBMITTED BY:
Frank Hilliard, East Liverpool

Poor Man's Cake

DIRECTIONS

Preheat oven to 350 degrees. Mix sugar, raisins, salt, cinnamon, shortening and water in a large saucepan. Boil 3 to 5 minutes. Cool. Add flour and baking soda to cooled mixture. Stir thoroughly. Pour into greased tube pan. Bake for 1 hour. Remove from pan and cool on rack.

INGREDIENTS

2 cups sugar

2 cups raisins

1 teaspoon salt

2 tablespoons cinnamon

2 tablespoons shortening

2 cups water

3 cups flour

1 teaspoon baking soda

SUBMITTED BY:
Denise Pearson, Russell

Puto or Philippine Steamed Bread

DIRECTIONS

Stir dry ingredients together (flour through sugar). Lightly beat together eggs, oil and milk. Stir liquid mixture into dry ingredients. Pour into buttered 9-inch square or round pan. Sprinkle anise seed on batter. Set on a rack over a pot of boiling water (or a high-dome electric frying pan set at boiling) and steam for 20 to 25 minutes. Butter top while hot and serve.

INGREDIENTS

2 cups flour

2 1/2 teaspoons baking powder

1/4 to 1/2 teaspoon salt

1/4 cup sugar

1 egg, beaten

1/3 cup canola oil

1 1/4 cup milk

1/2 teaspoon anise seed

Butter, for serving

SUBMITTED BY:

Pepita Jacobs, Indiana

Reese's Peanut Butter Cake

DIRECTIONS

Preheat oven to 350 degrees. In mixer, add cake mix, pudding mix, water, oil and eggs. Mix on low until moistened; then mix on high for 2 minutes. Add peanut butter cups and mix an additional 30 seconds. Pour in a 9x13-inch cake pan that has been sprayed with nonstick cooking spray. Bake 45 to 50 minutes or until toothpick inserted in middle comes out clean. Cool completely.

To make frosting, mix together peanut butter, cream cheese and powdered sugar in mixing bowl. Then mix in whipped topping. Mix until all ingredients are well combined. Frost cake. Top with peanut butter cups that have been crumbled.

NOTE

The peanut butter cups crumble better when refrigerated for 1 hour.

INGREDIENTS

1 (18 1/4-ounce) milk chocolate cake mix

1 (3.9-ounce) box instant chocolate pudding

1 1/2 cups water

1/3 cup oil

3 eggs, slightly beaten

10 (.6-ounce) peanut butter cups, broken into pieces

FROSTING:

3 tablespoons peanut butter

1 (8-ounce) package cream cheese, softened

3 1/4 cup powdered sugar

1 (8-ounce) container whipped topping, thawed

6 (.6-ounce) peanut butter cups, crumbled

SUBMITTED BY:
Christine Clark, Apollo

America's
HOME COOKING

Saucey Peach Cobbler

DIRECTIONS

Preheat oven to 375 degrees. Coat a 9-inch square or deep pie pan with vegetable cooking spray. Add the margarine and set aside. In another bowl, drain the peaches, reserve 1/2 cup of the juice and set aside. Combine flour, baking powder and 1/2 cup sugar in another bowl. Add 1/2 cup peach juice and milk. Stir well. Pour batter over the margarine in the baking dish. Spoon peaches and any remaining juice over batter. Sprinkle with the 3 table-spoons sugar. Do not stir. Bake for 35 to 40 minutes or until golden brown. (The peaches will sink to the bottom and form a sauce while the batter comes to the top.) Cut into wedges and serve warm. Good with ice cream, milk or whipped topping. Serves 6.

INGREDIENTS

1/4 cup melted margarine

2 (16-ounce) cans sliced peaches, drained

3/4 cup flour

1 teaspoon baking powder

1/2 cup plus 3 tablespoons sugar

1/4 cup milk

Ice cream, milk or whipped topping, for serving

SUBMITTED BY:
Frank Hilliard, East Liverpool

America's
HOME COOKING

Spritz Cookies

DIRECTIONS

Preheat oven to 350 degrees. Combine flour, sugar and salt in a food processor. Add shortening and butter; pulse to combine. Add eggs and vanilla; process until dough comes together. Chill dough for 1 hour. Put dough through cookie press onto lightly greased cookie sheets. Decorate as desired with jimmies, sprinkles, colored sugar, etc. Bake for 10 to 12 minutes or until the bottoms are just barely starting to brown.

NOTE

A few drops of food coloring also may be added to the dough.

INGREDIENTS

2 1/2 cups flour
2/3 cups sugar
Pinch of salt
1/2 cup shortening
1/2 cup butter
2 eggs
1 teaspoon vanilla

SUBMITTED BY:
Susan Cohen, Pittsburgh

Strawberry Dream Dessert

DIRECTIONS

Break up angel food cake into bite-sized pieces. Beat together milk, pudding and almond extract. Refrigerate for 5 minutes. Meanwhile, slice strawberries. Place in medium bowl and sprinkle with sugar. In a large bowl, layer cake pieces, pudding, strawberries and whipped topping. Repeat for another layer. Garnish top with additional strawberry slices, if desired.

INGREDIENTS

1 prepared angel food cake

3 cups milk

2 (3-ounce) boxes instant vanilla pudding mix

1 tablespoon almond extract

1 pint strawberries

2 tablespoons sugar

1 (8-ounce) container whipped topping, thawed

SUBMITTED BY:
Mickey Remich, New Kensington

America's
HOME COOKING

215

Index

Grandma Rutherford's Checkerboard Biscuits 18

Grandma Tippy-Toe's Swiss Steak 110

Grandma's Apple Butter Pie 194

Grandma's French Dressing 42

Grandma's Meatloaf 111

Grandma's Nut Rolls 195

Grandma's Vegetable Soup 43

Great Aunt Margaret Tarr's Cheesy Vegetables 157

Green Bean and Potato Soup 44

Grossmutter's Schmerkase Pie . . .196

H

Haluski Drop Dumplings (Grated Potatoes) .67

Ham Balls 112

Ham Hawaiian 113

Ham Loaf 114

Hobo Stew 115

Honeyed Applesauce 197

Huffle Puffle 116

Hungarian Butter 19

I

Italian Green Beans 158

Italian Macaroni Salad 45

Italian Shepherd Pie 117

J

Johnny Mayette, Revisited 118

K

Karin's Chicken Divan 119

*Kennywood Picnic City Chicken Sticks 120

Key Lime Pie 198

Killarney Bread 199

L

Langostino Corn Chowder 46

Leeks with Olive Oil (a la Turk) . . .159

Lemon Glazed Fruit Salad 47

Lemon Zucchini Bread 200

Lime Cheese Salad 48

M

Mandel Bread 201

Mazetti 121

Meatloaf Japanese Style 122

* Recipes were prepared on "America's Home Cooking: Family Favorites"

Index

Mint Chocolate Angel Food
Cake 202

Missouri 123

Molasses Sugar Cookies 203

Mom's Zucchini Casserole 160

Mustard Chicken or One-Pot
Chicken 124

N

*Nanna's Eggplant Patties 161

Ninety-Minute Dinner Rolls 204

Nonna's Broccoli and Pasta 68

Noodle Bake 69

Noodle Pudding 205

Nutty Baked French Toast 20

O

Old-Fashioned Potato Salad 49

Onions Oliver 162

Oven-Fried Chicken 125

P

Palachinka (Croatian Crepes) 206

Pan De Elote 126

Pancake in the Oven 21

Paprika Schnitzel 127

Party Sausage 22

Pastor Matt's Shepherd Pie 128

Peanut Butter Pie 207

Penne Alla Noci 70

Perogie Casserole 71

*Pignoli Cookies 208

Pineapple Casserole 23

Polish Pound Cake 209

Polpette .129

Poor Man's Cake 210

Pork Chops with Ketchup 130

Pork Snitzel 131

Pork-Q-Pine Balls 132

Potato Balls 72

Potato Dumplings and Kraut 73

Potato Latkes 74

Puto or Philippine Steamed
Bread 211

R

Real Gone Barbecued Pot
Roast 133

Reese's Peanut Butter Cake 212

Rice Pilaf .75

* Recipes were prepared on "America's Home Cooking: Family Favorites"

Index

Ricotta Gnocchi 76

Ricotta Sauce with Walnuts 77

Rigatoni with Spinach-Ricotta
Filling 78

Risotto 79

S

Saturday Buried Treasure 134

Saucy Peach Cobbler 213

Sauerkraut Balls 24

Sauerkraut Casserole 135

Scalloped Potatoes 80

Scalloped Potatoes Parmesan 81

*Scrippelles (Crepes) 82

Sicilian Steak 136

Sister Mary Francis' Potatoes 83

Slow Cooked Glazed Ham 137

Spaghetti Casserole 84

Spaghetti Pizza 85

Spanish Rice 86

Special Spinach Salad 50

*Spiedini .138

Spinach Dip 25

Spritz Cookies 214

Steak, Bacon & Macaroni 139

Strawberry Dream Dessert 215

Stuffed Bread 140

Stuffed Artichokes 163

Stuffed Cabbage 141

Stuffed French Toast 26

Stuffed Peppers European
Style 142

Sugar Cookies with Icing 216

Sunny Strawberry Soup 217

Sweet Potato Casserole 87

Sweet and Sour Green Beans . . .164

Sweet and Sour Meatballs with
Cabbage 143

Swiss Smoked Turkey Bake 144

Szekely Gulyas 145

T

Taco Pie Quiche 27

Tangy Pork Chops 146

Texas Sheet Cake 218

Tortellini Soup 51

*Tortilla Espanola (Spanish
Omelet) .28

* Recipes were prepared on "America's Home Cooking: Family Favorites"

America's
HOME COOKING

Index

Turkey Lasagna 88

Turkey Sausage Wonton
Appetizer 29

Turkey Tetrazinni 147

Tuscan Sausage Soup 52

U

Unstuffed Cabbage Casserole . . .148

Upside Down Pizza Pie 149

V

Vegetable Bake 165

Vegetable Beef Soup 53

Veggie Potato Salad 54

W

White Chocolate Crunch 219

Y

Yummy Cake 220

Z

Zazvorniky (Slovak Ginger
Cookies) 221

* Recipes were prepared on "America's Home Cooking: Family Favorites"

BREADWORKS™

QUALITY

★ ★ ★ ★ ★ ★ ★

A Pittsburgh Tradition

BAKERY AND STORE ★ OPEN 7 DAYS

412-231-7555

2110 Brighton Road • North Side